EXCELLENCE

Virender Kapoor is a thinker, an educationist and an inspirational guru. An alumnus of IIT Bombay and the former director of a prestigious management institute under the Symbiosis umbrella, he is currently the founder-director, president and chief mentor of Management Institute of Leadership and Excellence (MILE), Pune. His books on emotional intelligence, leadership and self-help have been translated into several regional and foreign languages. To know more about him, log on to www.virenderkapoor.com or mail him at virenderkapoor21@yahoo.com

Other books in the series:

Speaking: The Modi Way
Leadership: The Gandhi Way
Innovation: The Einstein Way

EXCELLENCE
THE AMITABH BACHCHAN WAY

VIRENDER KAPOOR

RUPA

Published by
Rupa Publications India Pvt. Ltd 2017
7/16, Ansari Road, Daryaganj
New Delhi 110002

Sales Centres:

Allahabad Bengaluru Chennai
Hyderabad Jaipur Kathmandu
Kolkata Mumbai

ISBN: 978-81-291-XXXX-X

First impression 2017

10 9 8 7 6 5 4 3 2 1

The moral right of the author has been asserted.

Printed at XXXXXX

CONTENTS

PREFACE

*'Style is a reflection of your attitude and
your personality.'*

—Shawn Ashmore

Writing a book on Amitabh Bachchan has been extremely difficult. At the same time, it has also been very easy. It was a challenge because a lot has already been written about this man who has been in the limelight for the past four decades. Is there anything left to be told that a reader might be interested in—or better—may be able to learn something from? On the other hand, it was easy because there is so much to learn from this individual that one can easily create impactful content for the audience. Each of his interviews with the media are words that impart wisdom—with nuggets of inspiration for each one of us.

His performances in the movies are awe-inspiring and each episode of *Kaun Banega Crorepati* left a lasting impression on millions of people across the world. I have often asked my students one question, 'Given a choice, would you be an Ambani or an Amitabh? One has a lot of money but little fame, while the other has immense fame but little money.' Amitabh is the usual response. If you ask me, I would also vote for Amitabh.

Does this adulation only exist because of his popularity, fan following, acting and panache or is there something more to it? Certainly, there is a lot more than just that. Along with great acting, there are multiple facets of his personality that are hard to miss. After all, there is always so much to learn from people who have gone through different phases of life— the good, the bad and the ugly. In his case, however, the situations have been the best, the worst and the most horrid. It requires a lot of determination, willpower and patience to manage the ups and downs of an unpredictable film career, combined with health issues and a failed business venture. Handling challenging roles and delivering your 100 per cent to satisfy people via a medium that opens you to constant scrutiny and keeps you under a microscope all the time—frame by frame—is not a small achievement. Though film-making is teamwork, film actors are lone rangers who need to stand on their own two feet to either perform or perish. It is a known fact that audiences are unforgiving. They can send you fan mails and hate mails at the same frenzied pace. It is, therefore, important to take both in one's stride. And let's admit it, Amitabh Bachchan does have big strides!

For me, he is the perfect example of demonstrative excellence. It is not difficult to find almost every quality one requires to excel in Amitabh Bachchan and that is the best thing to learn from this enigmatic personality. It also happens to be the best thing to write about him.

I found what to write about—so obvious, so true and yet not explored and explained in the correct perspective. You feel the sun's energy all the time, yet you require a magnifying glass to channelize it and light a fire. This megastar has the sun's energy. This is what I feel was required to be written about; this is what was missing.

When you talk about IQ—Intelligence Quotient—you think of Albert Einstein. But when you talk of Emotional Quotient and human excellence, which role model do you think of to illustrate the point? Who would be better than Big B for this role? In the Indian cinema, I can't think of anyone else. So, let's cast him right away.

INTRODUCTION

Excellence, the Power Within

*'Excellence is never an accident. It is always the result
of high intention, sincere effort, and intelligent execution;
it represents the wise choice of many alternatives—choice,
not chance, determines your destiny.'*

—Aristotle

Traditionally, the analysts looked at human competence through a very small window. IQ was the de facto measure of human excellence for a very long time, almost throughout the last century. It was based on mathematical deduction, logical reasoning and linguistic prowess, and therefore, the tests were also devised accordingly.

The reason for this bias towards logical and scientific reasoning was not ill-founded. The last century was marked by scientific discoveries and inventions based on physics, chemistry, mathematics and biology. Those were the days of steam engines, cars, discovery of penicillin, medical research, aircraft, quantum mechanics, rockets and telephony as well as electricity. Our development and progress depended on these sciences. Even war supremacy during the two world wars was determined by more effective weaponry conceived first in laboratories and later manufactured in more efficient factories. That, of course, is true even today.

Scientific prowess in those days, therefore, was very sought after. If you did not excel in the sciences or math, you were deemed not good enough. As a result, the brightest students opted for science, the not-so-bright went for economics and commerce, while the rest had to be content with taking up arts as their academic stream.

Importance of the Latent Human Abilities for Success

Gradually, the new world order saw the emergence of a service sector and developed nations moved towards softer skills required in these areas. Scientists and analysts started realizing the potential of 'other' human skills which had existed before but had never been appreciated. This realization dawned upon the scientific community almost at the end of the last century.

Emotional Intelligence became the new measure for human excellence. These seemingly intangible skills began appearing as some of the most important human assets. Driven and defined by self-awareness, self-management, social awareness and relationship management, Emotional Intelligence emerged as a new tool to predict the success of an individual. Almost at the same time, the multiple intelligence theory—a still broader view—was put forth by Howard Gardner (American Developmental Scientist at Harvard) who studied human competence across a larger spectrum with seven intelligences in place. These seven intelligences are: linguistic, musical, logical-mathematical, spatial (including dance and acting), kinesthetic, interpersonal-personal and intrapersonal—the last two are covered by Emotional Intelligence.

I would like to compartmentalize these seven intelligences into three basic blocks:

The first is the traditional IQ-based competence in which linguistic and logical-mathematical intelligences are included. Linguistic intelligence takes into account one's ability to deal with languages effectively—creating lyrics, poetry and storytelling. In a nutshell, it is the mastery of syntax, whatever the language may be.

The second block consists of the gifted domain—musical, bodily kinesthetic and spatial intelligences.

The third block is the Emotional Intelligence block which caters to intrapersonal and interpersonal intelligence—resilience, mental toughness, handling failures effectively, dealing appropriately with people, managing moods and emotions like anger and empathy. Networking and integrity have nothing to do with your IQ or your ability to sing and dance. These are traits which equip us with self-awareness and self-management as well as the capability to understand others and manage our relationships. This is the intelligence of excellence. Without its support, the previous two blocks cannot be fully utilized by any individual.

Allow me to explain. Let us take the example of a boy who possesses logical and mathematical intelligence in abundance and has the potential to become a top-notch engineer or a scientist of great calibre. If this boy does not prepare for his competitive exams diligently, he will fail to qualify. He needs to work hard, balance his moods, listen to his coach, possess self-control and manage his time properly to achieve that. In other words, he won't be able to excel just with the help of a high IQ. That is exactly what excellence is about.

Similarly, a great cricket player will fail as a captain if he is unable to control his own emotions, show empathy towards other team players, or if he ignores their problems, strengths and weaknesses. Above all, he should be able to withstand pressure.

The same goes for an actor. If as an actor, you do not work on your role, ignore the director, remain dishonest with your work, overestimate yourself and assume that you know everything, you may not go very far. It is essential to be courteous to your co-stars and fans, and exhibit professionalism in terms of punctuality and sincerity.

Therefore, possessing abilities defined by block one and block two are very important but not backing these with skills in block three can be disastrous. Brilliant engineers have failed, great actors have perished and promising players couldn't make it—simply because they could not handle themselves in their new surroundings.

It has been summed up quite appropriately by Aristotle, 'A virtue or excellence is a character trait, acquired by practice that disposes a person to adopt the right course of action in morally charged situations. Virtues are life skills that enable a person to realize their potential for living the good life as a rational, social animal.'

Human excellence, thus, can be defined as a cluster of qualities due to which an individual stands out exceptionally superior to others and it allows him to be the best in the field of human endeavours and activities. This is the intelligence of excellence. Throughout this book, I will use Emotional Intelligence and excellence interchangeably.

Amitabh Bachchan possesses not only the kinesthetic, linguistic and musical intelligences but also has abilities which are enshrined in the continuum of excellence. These have contributed majorly towards his success as an actor, professional and a good human being.

Worldly Abilities That Helped Him Excel

There is a lot one can learn from him in the broad arena of worldly skills and this book attempts to touch upon some of his most valuable qualities. Let us briefly examine his attributes:

1. Handling pain and failure: This is one quality which is extremely important in a competitive world. Amitabh Bachchan, during his 50-year-long career, has seen ups and downs which very few have experienced. A serious injury during the shooting of the movie *Coolie* (1983) and several other health issues which nag him even today would have taken a toll on any other person. Despite serious health-related issues, this man stood the test of time and gave his best to his directors and audience each and every time he performed. Meeting deadlines, managing difficult weather conditions during outdoor shootings and

handling dubbing schedules at odd times with bad health is not easy. Acting is very different from an office job; you are always exposed to a camera which can capture your minutest discomfort. This man did all of it and that too, with his chin up.

2. Self-discipline: Discipline and meticulousness are two of the most important professional traits. Without these, you cannot survive in a competitive environment, especially in the cinema industry where there is cutthroat competition. Amitabh Bachchan is professional, self-disciplined and cooperative with his directors and co-stars. He handles every assignment diligently. He feels that if he is being paid for a job, he must deliver his best to the directors and producers.

3. Respect for time: He is known for his punctuality in the industry. Despite being successful for a very long time, he has never disregarded punctuality or thrown any tantrums on the sets. He has always been on time for every shoot, even during the busiest days when he was doing three shifts a day for different movies. Once, he was seen running on the road—with his car stuck in a traffic jam—just so he could be on time for a function.

4. Appreciating others: It is not easy to appreciate your co-stars when you have reached the zenith of your career. Most people are not able to handle success and, therefore, become arrogant, conceited and even rude to their juniors. But not him. He has always admired others' work and has maintained a cordial behaviour with everyone he has worked with.

5. Panache and grace: Grace under pressure is a quality only great people and professionals possess. Amitabh Bachchan has handled tremendous pressure extraordinarily, even when his career graph was not looking too good and his business venture was in the doldrums. He demonstrated the rare capability of taking the blow on the chin without a single complaint.

6. Integrity and value system: Mr Bachchan has always demonstrated respect for elders and family values. His genuine courtesy with his co-stars is something one cannot miss about him.

7. Accepting your weaknesses: When his company Amitabh Bachchan Corporation Ltd. (ABCL) was in deep financial trouble, he never put the blame on anyone else. He accepted that he had not acted with good business and financial sense. When asked for his opinion about the industry that did not support him in his worst time, he clearly mentioned that it would have been impossible for someone else to bail him out of his own mistakes.

8. Philanthropy, empathy and giving back to society: He may not have donated big bucks to charity but he has always supported government projects like 'Save the Tiger' and campaigns for tuberculosis and polio awareness. He has stood by the farmers who were on the verge of committing suicide. At many instances, he has also helped his senior co-stars financially.

9. Bouncing back after failure: Whether it was his illness, failed business or a bad phase in his career, he has demonstrated courage and has fought back fiercely after

every failure to emerge as a winner.

10. Humility and style: In every interview, he seems humble and down to earth. Even during his public appearances or in the KBC episodes, the man has always demonstrated élan and courtesy with all the participants.

1

FROM ORDINARY TO EXTRAORDINARY

Sketch of an Actor and a Gentleman

'Being male is a matter of birth.
Being a man is a matter of age.
But being a gentleman is a matter of choice.'

—Vin Diesel

Born on 11 October 1942 in Allahabad, Uttar Pradesh, to a family of teachers, scholars, performing art enthusiasts, writers and poets, Amitabh Bachchan was raised in an intellectually rich and diverse environment. His father, Harivansh Rai Srivastava, taught English while his mother, born as Teji Suri (Punjabi Sikh) taught psychology. Mr Harivansh Rai was called 'bachchan' (a kid) at home and later, when he was pursuing his PhD in English literature at Cambridge, he started using 'Bachchan' instead of Srivastava as his last name. It became his pen name for the rest of his life. He contributed to Hindi literature immensely and was a writer and poet of eminence. He has even translated works of greats like Shakespeare in Hindi.

Amitabh was initially named Inquilaab but on the suggestion of his father's close friend, it was changed to Amitabh which means a light that will never die. He did his schooling from Sherwood College, Nainital, and later attended Kirori Mal College, University of Delhi. He worked as a business executive with multinational companies in Calcutta (now Kolkata) for a few years before turning towards fine arts. He shared accommodation with his colleagues and lived a frugal life as that was all he could afford in those days with a salary of 500 rupees per month. He made several good friends and spent a number of years in the city which he loves even today.

He tried his hand at theatre and also wanted to contribute to the national public radio broadcaster of India, All India Radio, but he was rejected as they found his voice unsuitable. However, he finally got his first break in cinema as a narrator in Mrinal Sen's National Award-winning film *Bhuvan Shome* (1969). It was a very small assignment for which he was paid around 300 rupees.

His first acting role was in the film *Saat Hindustani* (1969), directed by Khwaja Ahmad Abbas, featuring Utpal Dutt and Jalal Agha. There was no big launch or fancy debut performance for him. Initially, several of his films did badly at the box office, not benefitting his performance graph much. Anyone in his position would have quit after facing so many disappointments. But he held on.

From 1969 to 1973, he made special appearances and

played small roles in various films. His performance in Hrishikesh Mukherjee's film *Anand* (1971), in which he played a doctor's role alongside the then superstar Rajesh Khanna, won him the Filmfare Award for Best Supporting Actor. His performance was so measured, impactful and precise that no one could miss out the brilliant actor in him. Rajesh Khanna, a superstar in those days, said, 'Watch out for this man…he will do very well.'

By now, he was confident and had managed to make a mark in the acting arena. He started as an actor, not as a star. He delivered some great performances in films like *Guddi* (1971), *Parwana* (1971) and *Bombay to Goa* (1972), before hitting the jackpot with *Zanjeer* (1973), a Prakash Mehra venture in which he played the lead role of a no-nonsense police inspector. It was because of this role that the concept of 'angry young man' got popularized. He got married to Jaya Bhaduri in 1973, after the release of *Zanjeer*.

In a creative field, especially in cinema, I feel that several windows must open together for one to gain stardom and bag a super hit film. For instance, Rajesh Khanna's luck turned around with *Aradhana* (1969), directed by the veteran film-maker Shakti Samantha. The music by S.D. Burman and R.D. Burman combined with a romantic-emotional storyline by Sachin Bhowmick worked well for the audience in those days. The songs in the movie were sung by Kishore Kumar whose voice suited Rajesh Khanna's personality perfectly. As they say, everything fell in place.

Similarly, *Zanjeer* opened these windows for Amitabh Bachchan. A brilliant script as if written especially for him by Salim-Javed; an excellent screenplay, music by Kalyanji-Anandji and lyrics by Gulshan Bawra—all these factors brought together a unique concept for the masses when all people wanted was a change from lovey-dovey scenes to action-packed performances. Pran, Ajit Khan, Om Prakash, Bindu and Iftekhar completed this power-packed film. This movie got Amitabh nominated for another Filmfare Award. He was now a part of mainstream commercial cinema.

Another very important thing responsible for success in film industry is the temperament of the audience which changes with time. For instance, there was a flood of war movies in the '50s and early '60s as the world had just gotten out of World War II. Hollywood also churned out great movies related to war in the early '70s. *For a Few Dollars More* (1965), *The Good, the Bad and the Ugly* (1966) and *Mackenna's Gold* (1969) can never be written off our memories. Directors and storytellers must know the mood of the nation and the trends across the world to pick up a subject relevant to the times. During those days, there was a rebellious fervour in the air and people wanted an action hero to fight against the evil, the bad and the corrupt. Of course, romance and comedy existed too. But there was more demand for action-packed movies. For Amitabh Bachchan, this transformation of the nation's mood was a godsend.

It is true that an actor simply enacts a story but good fortune is also required to get the right script at the right time. From here onwards, there was no looking back. His performances in movies like *Abhimaan* (1973), *Namak Haraam* (1973), *Deewaar* (1975), *Sholay* (1975), *Chupke Chupke* (1975),

Kabhi Kabhie (1976), *Don* (1978), *Kaala Patthar* (1979), *Mr. Natwarlal* (1979), *Silsila* (1981), *Laawaris* (1981), *Satte Pe Satta* (1982) and *Sharaabi* (1984) in the coming years not only gave him a huge box office presence but also allowed him to experiment with different roles, ranging from an angry young man to romance and comedy. He performed exceptionally well in every role he was offered to play.

Unfortunately, his good fortune did not last long. He was badly hurt on the sets of *Coolie* while shooting an action scene in Bangalore (now Bengaluru). It caused a serious injury and he was hospitalized for several months. It was a close shave with death and the entire nation prayed for his recovery. He was later diagnosed with myasthenia gravis, a rare muscular disease which, in some cases, can become progressively degenerative. He was already suffering from asthma and this illness was a big impediment to his performance. He talked about his troubles with the *Times of India* correspondent, Khalid Mohamed. He mentioned how he knew he was very ill and was not sure if he would ever be able to face the camera again. In one of his interviews, he revealed that it was difficult to even change clothes and comb his hair. For a while, he became pessimistic and apprehensive about his films. Before the release of every film, he would express concern about how the new film would be received and was often heard saying, '*Yeh film toh flop hogi!*' (This film will flop.)

An actor's life is not a bed of roses contrary to what many might believe. Film actors have to work very hard, travel extensively in different climatic conditions and wear all sorts of costumes and make-up which can be difficult to handle over a prolonged period, even for a healthy person. Moreover, some actors rise to fame and disappear very quickly. An actor, therefore, gets his chance only when the right windows open and he has to make the best of the opportunities at that very point. An illness can never be a part of the plan.

Film industry works in three shifts—morning shift (7 a.m. to 2 p.m.), afternoon shift (2 p.m. to 10 p.m.) and night shift (10 p.m. to 6 a.m.). Bollywood never sleeps. Successful actors at the peak of their careers often shoot on all the three shifts of the day. They may curse the gruelling routine but getting offers is good news. Being in demand is a complement they cannot ignore. Amitabh Bachchan tasted success after a lot of struggle. And when he finally did, he wanted to give his best, even on the days when he was in high demand. He was shooting for almost three shifts a day when he was at the peak of his career which literally meant 24/7 work. It was a tough time for him as after his injury, the routine got more exhausting. Like every other human being, he felt the tremendous strain. Yet as I mentioned earlier, being busy is a 'trophy of agony' which every actor likes to flaunt, not realizing its long-term impact on one's health. Amitabh Bachchan took this professional hazard in his stride and in his blog, he wrote, 'Damn, I am so busy, I am doing three shifts a day!' But as they say, when the going gets tough, the tough get going. Amitabh Bachchan did just that. You require courage and internal strength to fight the physical challenges of illness. He demonstrated the power of mind over body perfectly.

But it is not as if he did not suffer pain or anxiety. He just managed it well most of the times. About his battle with his body, he is of the opinion that we all go through pain at some time or the other in our lives, but whether we allow ourselves to suffer as a result of that is our choice. He reflects on this a little philosophically in his blog, '*Hai andheri raat par diya jalana kab mana hai?*' (Yes, it is a dark night, but when has anyone stopped you from lighting a lamp?)

So, pain cannot be avoided but prolonged suffering due to the pain is often not required. Bear it and live with it but never let it overcome you. Emotional Intelligence has a lot to do with self-management. It is about soothing yourself during a crisis.

One of the other challenges of cinema and acting is that one has to dub their own dialogues for most of the portions shot earlier. Obviously, the director as well as the actor wants his/her voice to sound the best for every shot and frame. Therefore, it is something unavoidable.

The challenge, however, is the huge gap between the dubbing and the actual shooting of a scene and the fact that dubbing happens without the props and the environment in which the scene was initially shot.

Mr Bachchan explained the difficulty in his blog by admitting how re-enacting a moment in front of a microphone with the right emotions was an onerous task. He also revealed that the most daunting aspect of the process was realizing that the performance was going to be judged later not by what one did in front of the camera but by how one performed in a sanitized recording studio in front of a mic. But it had to be done and he always did it without fuss.

In 1984, Amitabh Bachchan took a break from acting and

briefly entered politics in support of his old family friend, Rajiv Gandhi. He won Allahabad's seat of the eighth Lok Sabha after defeating H.N. Bahuguna, the former chief minister of Uttar Pradesh. He won with a very high margin but was unfortunately dragged into the Bofors scandal later. Though he was declared not guilty, he resigned after three years as he realized he was not cut out for politics.

His return to films after a short encounter with politics was with *Shahenshah* (1988). It was a box office success. But after the tremendous hit, his subsequent movies did not do well. *Gangaa Jamunaa Saraswathi* (1988), *Toofan* (1989), *Jaadugar* (1989) and *Main Azaad Hoon* (1989)—none of the movies were appreciated by the people despite his noteworthy performance in *Main Azaad Hoon*. Even the National Film Award he received for *Agneepath* (1990) couldn't get him back to his original position. He got his third Filmfare Award for *Hum* (1991) but soon after that, he went into hibernation for almost five years.

In 1996, he started a business venture by setting up Amitabh Bachchan Corporation Limited (ABCL). It had plans to become a \$250 million company in the next five years. The business model included a variety of products and services related to the entertainment industry like production, distribution of films and event management. Few films the likes of *Tere Mere Sapne* (1996), *Ullaasam* (1997) and *Major Saab* (1998) produced by ABCL failed to do well at the box office. Amitabh Bachchan relaunched himself with *Mrityudaata* (1997), also produced by ABCL, but that too did not excel financially. The real problems began when ABCL became the main sponsor of the 1996 Miss World beauty pageant held in Bangalore. It lost so much money that it led to Amitabh's financial collapse in 1997. There were legal battles and his bungalow was mortgaged in order to raise money for the loans taken on the account of the beauty pageant. Amar Singh of the Samajwadi Party supported him morally during this financial crisis. Jaya Bachchan too joined the Samajwadi Party and represented it in the Rajya Sabha as a member of the parliament. Desperate to fight back, Bachchan tried movies like *Lal Baadshah* (1999), *Kohram* (1999) and *Sooryavansham* (1999) with other production houses but failed to achieve much.

After a series of failures and financial losses enough to last him a lifetime, the year 2000 brought about a refreshing change for Amitabh Bachchan. The beginning of the decade was productive and important for him. He made a comeback with Yash Chopra's *Mohabbatein* (2000) which won him his third Filmfare Award for Best Supporting Actor. This was followed by a series of hits like *Kabhi Khushi Kabhie Gham...* (2001), *Baghban* (2003) and *Black* (2005). He played a range of characters and demonstrated his versatility in movies like *Aks* (2001), *Khakee* (2004) and *Dev* (2004). The launch of the TV game show *Kaun Banega Crorepati* (KBC) made him a household name because of its instant success. The format of the show was different and so was his suave performance.

Successful films coupled with KBC improved his image in the minds of the audience and the cash registers started ringing once again for him. He was now a sought-after actor and was offered numerous commercial product advertisements on TV, print media and hoardings. And he did it all flawlessly.

The success story continued for the next half of the decade as well as with films like *Bunty Aur Babli* (2005), *Sarkar* (2005), *Kabhi Alvida Naa Kehna* (2006), *Cheeni Kum* (2007), the multi-starrer *Shootout at Lokhandwala* (2007), *Bhoothnath* (2008) and *Paa* (2009) which won him his third National Film and fifth Filmfare Awards for Best Actor.

In the next decade too, Amitabh Bachchan continued reinventing himself with greater and more versatile performances. He played a father suffering from constipation in *Piku* (2015) which won him his fourth National Film and third Filmfare Critics Awards for Best Actor. His Hollywood debut opposite Leonardo DiCaprio and Tobey Maguire in *The Great Gatsby* (2013) was also well-appreciated. One of his latest movies, *Pink* (2016) was a huge success, earning over 100 crores at the box office. It also set a new trend in the Indian cinema.

Such reversal of circumstances is not a small accomplishment. A second chance was offered to him when he was around 60 and he worked tirelessly. His advertisement assignments increased manifold which demanded more of his time. If one has to learn the meaning and spirit of bouncing back after failure and resilience; there is no better role model than Amitabh Bachchan. Not satisfied with one career, he tried his hand at many things. Apart from mainstream cinema and TV, he sang multiple songs and lent his voice to several film projects such as *Lagaan* (2001), *Jodhaa Akbar* (2008), *Kahaani* (2012) and *Mahabharat* (2013). A person who was rejected by

All India Radio because of poor quality of voice began to be well-known for his baritone. Today, he can proudly say, 'Meri Awaaz He Meri Pehchan Hai.' (My voice is my identity.) He also lent his voice to the Oscar-winning French documentary *March of the Penguins* (2005), directed by Luc Jacquet.

Apart from Filmfare and National Awards, he has won many other accolades. In 2001, he was honoured with the Actor of the Century Award at the Alexandria International Film Festival in Egypt for his contribution to the world of cinema. He was the first artist to receive the Filmfare Lifetime Achievement Award which was established in the name of Raj Kapoor. He was crowned Superstar of the Millennium in 2000 at the Filmfare Award ceremony. In June 2000, he also became the first living Asian to have a wax statute at London's Madame Tussauds wax museum. His statues were also installed in New York, Hong Kong, Bangkok and Washington, D.C. To add to the long list, he is a recipient of Padma Shri (1984), Padma Bhushan (2001) and Padma Vibhushan (2015), bestowed by the Government of India. For his exceptional career in the world of cinema, he was also conferred upon the Knight of the Legion of Honour, the highest civilian honour given by the French government.

It is, therefore, safe to conclude that Amitabh Bachchan's journey is nothing short of inspirational. He started with no background in the film industry and made it to the top on his own. He had his share of ups and downs throughout his career but he sailed through. A career that has survived for more than four decades and is still ticking—it is a true case of *Kabhie Khushie Kabhie Gham* in real life. Fame, money—both excess and lack of it—and ill health were handled simultaneously by him in his life. He maintained his calm and humility all along. This is nothing but an ideal demonstration of tenacity, willpower and resilience by the gentleman—a symbol of excellence.

> *'Life isn't about finding yourself.*
> *Life is about creating yourself.'*
>
> —George Bernard Shaw

2

PUNCTUALITY, RESPONSIVENESS AND PROMPTNESS

In Pursuit of the 25th Hour

*'If you have been told that you are late and unreliable
more than once, then not only do you lack punctuality,
but you also lack decency and seriousness,
which is certainly very annoying.'*

—Auliq Ice

In the chaotic world we live in, managing our time effectively is a big challenge for all of us. We all have so much to do and so much to not do that we hardly ever know the difference between right and wrong. Did I say 'so much to not do'? Yes, you read that right. Not to WhatsApp, Facebook, text, tweet, chat, hang around, engage in long infructuous phone calls—they should be on our 'Not To Do' list.

Activities mentioned above cause self-inflicted injuries to our own time. When I say our own time, I am referring to the precious time that really belongs to each one of us. That time is limited by the number of years allotted to us by the divine power. A life span of 75 years translated into 39,420,000 minutes is what we get—quite literally. The first 15 years hardly count as we are still becoming the person we are meant to be and that leaves us with just 31,536,000 minutes in 60 odd years of our conscious living. Time, therefore, is the most perishable commodity. Yesterday will never come back, though there will always be a tomorrow.

This exhaustive calculation was for those who do not value time. Even though most of us understand that time is precious, we do not make efforts to manage it well. Is it difficult? Yes and no. 'Yes' for those who make conscious efforts to utilize their time and 'no' for those who don't care. It is that simple.

Can You Turn Chaos into an Organized Chaos?

There are certain professions which force you to live a chaotic life. Show business and the acting industry are some of these professions. Today, even entrepreneurs live in chaos. For such people, there are no nine to five jobs. They seem to have no control on their lives and their time. For them to remain punctual and manage their lives is more difficult than those who have a well-defined job description with the weekends thrown in as official time provided to relax. Today, with profit margins shrinking and tight control on headcount, corporate life is not easy. During an MBA course I was conducting, I made sure the students understood that the corporate life which they would soon experience would be very demanding and they would have to multitask, travel, brainstorm, discuss and make decisions almost simultaneously, with no breathing time in between. I ensured that the first year of the course was rigorous and students got the taste of working for at least 15 hours a day in the first semester itself. It helped them immensely when they took up their first corporate assignment.

Today, for most of the working class, the days are hectic, workload is unpredictable and days seem endless. To be more prepared to handle this kind of pressure, one needs to be organized, disciplined, punctual, responsive and prompt—only then can professional and personal obligations be met appropriately.

Amitabh Bachchan is one such person who is forced to live such a life. For actors too, there are peak times and periods of absolute lull but they need to dynamically shift gears to adjust their pace to the speed of chaos around them. These are the people who, with their sheer discipline and willpower, are 'chaotically organized'. They manage to turn life into an organized chaos!

Mr Bachchan writes his blog every day and the man even numbers the entries diligently with the exact day, date and time. Most of these comments are written in his free time or at night when he gets over with his shifts. Till date, he has written 3,411 blog entries and they usually follow the pattern mentioned below:

DAY 3411
Jalsa, Mumbai   July 30/31, 2017   Sun/Mon 2:20 am

He is also very active on Twitter and tweets purposefully. His comments are meaningful and relevant, imparting wisdom to the readers. I feel people who value time and are punctual have three things in common. First, they are disciplined; second, they have high self-esteem and do not like to embarrass themselves in front of others because of their tardiness; and third, they think it is discourteous to keep others waiting. Amitabh Bachchan possesses all these qualities. Punctuality is his trademark. It is a quality he admires in other people as well.

This is something he has mentioned time and again. When asked if he has any quality that one can learn from, he has often said that even though he thinks he doesn't have enough qualities to be copied, it is his punctuality that people can learn from.

'I owe all my success in life to having been always a quarter of an hour before my time.'

—Lord Nelson

People Appreciate Punctuality

Punctuality is appreciated by all but unfortunately in India; we don't bother to bother about it. In my teaching career where my job was to groom budding future managers, I would put a lot of stress on being on time. 9 a.m. was 8.55 a.m. by default in my institute. I used to emphasize so much on punctuality that from a habit, it became a reflex action for my students. I am a firm believer of the fact that in a nation which is so callous towards punctuality, anyone who is on time stands out like a bouquet of flowers and is appreciated by everyone.

I always tell my students and staff to make punctuality their USP—unique selling proposition—and it will help them stand out at a workplace. A consistent feedback from the industries where my students began working was that they were very punctual and were always well-dressed. Rain or shine, they never got late.

When you are punctual, people are in awe of you. During the British Raj, the British officers demonstrated punctuality at all times in front of their Indian staff. They impressed their subordinates with their respect for time. The impression 'Sahaab will never be late for any function, official or private' was deeply imbedded in every subordinate. I do not understand how we failed to inculcate this quality even when we were ruled by the British for decades. Most of our government offices are out of sync and they do not care for the fact that their callousness is a cause of pain for thousands of citizens who have to deal with them and are at their mercy for many things.

After Mr Modi became the prime minister of India, he ensured a sense of responsiveness and punctuality in the central government offices which were so used to the 'sab chalta hai' attitude. In the beginning, the babus and bureaucrats who have not had much respect for punctuality since the last '70 years of independence found it hard to change. Yet, with single-minded focus, Mr Modi ensured that it was done right from top to bottom.

Film industry, just like the bureaucracy, is notorious for its lack of punctuality. Star tantrums where actors—especially the successful ones—hold the director, producer and co-stars at ransom because 'they matter' are prevalent. It is not right to treat others like dirt and act as if no one else matters. This, I feel, reflects on an individual's upbringing and their lack of values and decency.

'Better three hours too soon than a minute too late.'

—William Shakespeare

Co-stars, directors and the media hold Mr Bachchan in very high esteem because of his respect for time. One journalist recalled that when he invited Mr Bachchan for his wedding reception, he was not expecting him because he knew that he had a very busy shooting schedule. But he was pleasantly surprised when Mr Bachchan showed up and that too, absolutely on time. His secretary had previously informed the journalist that he would arrive at 8.30 p.m. sharp and he reached at 8.25 p.m.—five minutes before time! Amitabh Bachchan is known for being courteous to such an extent that he makes all sorts of adjustments in his work schedule to accommodate appointments once he accepts them. He often reaches before others despite the fact that he is the biggest and the senior most star of the industry.

For a morning shift on sets which starts as early as 7 a.m., he usually lands up in the studio even before the gates are opened by the guards. While waiting, he sometimes waters the plants or just casually walks around. He once spent four hours waiting for Madhuri Dixit and when she arrived, he received her without a trace of annoyance on his face. This is what makes him larger than life and people respect him immensely in an industry fraught with snobbish actors and star tantrums.

Anupam Kher, when his career was at its zenith, would sometimes come late for shootings. Once he was shooting for the movie *Aakhree Raasta* (1986) in Chennai and the weather was sweltering. He reached almost an hour late and was annoyed with the people on the set because the air conditioner in the make-up room was not functioning properly. He was surprised to see Mr Bachchan sitting quietly with full make-up on in his costume which was a blanket, in accordance to what the scene demanded. He mentioned that he had been completely in awe of Big B when he had seen him sitting silently without any fuss. Kher admitted how he learnt an important lesson in punctuality and humility that day and decided to never throw tantrums in the future.

Pandit Hridaynath Mangeshkar, a noted music composer and singer, and the younger brother of Lata Mangeshkar introduced an award to honour a personality for his/her contribution to the society. Lata Mangeshkar chose Amitabh Bachchan over the likes of Sachin Tendulkar and A.P.J. Abdul Kalam. Mr Bachchan accepted this invitation and despite his busy schedule, he arrived right on time to receive the award.

I feel we have a lot to learn from this man. During his days in politics, he was a pain for his campaign managers as he was always on time for all the meetings and that was something the politicians were not used to. He was on time even on days when there were massive traffic jams on the roads. If due to any reason he ended up being late, he would publically apologize and make it up to the audience. Perhaps Amitabh Bachchan's huge collection of watches has a lot to do with his passion for time management!

According to me, being on time is not difficult provided we understand it as an obligatory requirement of a modern society. A little effort can make a lot of difference in how people eventually perceive us. After all, the impression we leave on people is ultimately in our hands.

Promptness, Politeness and Responsiveness Go a Long Way

Ulhas Shirke, a freelance writer in fitness and healthcare, shares some of his personal experiences with Mr Bachchan in his article on Magzmumbai.com. He recalls an incident when Amitabh Bachchan was asked to give a 'muhurat clap' at the Juhu bungalow. It was Govinda's film and the time given for the muhurat was 9.30 a.m. Amitabh arrived exactly at 9.25 a.m. and was there before Govinda who had not reached on time for the muhurat of his own movie. He had to wait for more than half an hour for his arrival. It was a source of great embarrassment for the film-makers and Govinda.

When Shirke wrote his book *Fitness and Beyond*, he sent Mr Bachchan a copy as he had written something about Big B in the book. He was pleasantly surprised to receive a letter of appreciation from him. It appeared as if he had read every page of the 188-page book. This was the level of promptness and time management exhibited by him at various occasions. Another unbelievable incident took place when he was getting late for an event as his car was stuck in a traffic jam. He got out of the car and almost ran with his bodyguards to cross over and reach the event on time.

During the making *of Bhoothnath Returns* (2014), Parth, Mr Bachchan's young co-star, was awestruck by Big B. He mentioned how despite being a star, he was on the sets before everyone and during breaks, he would sit and chat with him instead of going back to the vanity van. He said that Amitabh Bachchan was a gem of a person and always made him feel comfortable. He added that there were a lot of things one could learn from him.

Arjun Rampal, who has worked with Mr Bachchan, is all praises for him. He is of the opinion that Bachchan is the most generous actor he has ever worked with. In an interview with *Hindustan Times* on December 2016, he revealed that Mr Bachchan was not intimidating at all. He said that initially if one did not know him, one would perhaps feel intimidated out of respect, but he always made sure that people around him were at ease.

Dr T.V. Rao in his book *Effective People* described how in the movie *Paa*, to get into character, Bachchan had to spend four to five hours every day donning prosthetics and make-up, post which he could not eat or drink normally. He added that his interaction with his fans and the press was generally warm and gracious and he made visible efforts to remain humble and grounded. Despite the constant attention which can get to even the most patient people, he managed to keep his cool and handled the shutterbug invasion with a smile, posing for them and answering their questions.

Mr Bachchan played a short yet pivotal role in *The Great Gatsby* with the Hollywood star Leonardo DiCaprio in the lead role. Leonardo, during his interview with NDTV at Cannes, mentioned that Amitabh Bachchan was a gentle and wonderful individual to work with. DiCaprio thought he was exceptionally talented and appreciated the way Bachchan embodied the roughness and mystery of Meyer Wolfsheim. He was impressed with him behind the scenes as well and even thought that everything that came out of his mouth was filled with so much presence. He mentioned how Bachchan was a perfect gentleman and a wonderful collaborator, and he was honoured to have worked with him.

Little Things Matter

Amitabh Bachchan is also very particular and prompt when it comes to wishing people on occasions. In an interview with him, Ranbir Kapoor, who was the interviewer, revealed that Mr Bachchan had called him once on his birthday when he was pursuing his acting course abroad and he had been unable to take the call. He had then left a message on his voice mail wishing him a very happy birthday. Ranbir Kapoor joked about how he had made all his friends listen to that message because it had genuinely made his day.

Small things like this matter a lot in the long run. Great people have great ways of doing things and no one does it better than Big B.

'The while we keep a man waiting,
he reflects on our shortcomings.'

—French Proverb

Respect for Colleagues and Seniors

During Amitabh Bachchan's initial days of struggle, Rajesh Khanna was already a superstar and could get away with anything. He often threw tantrums and was never on time for shootings. This was quite a problem for his co-stars and producers who were spending a huge amount of money on the sets. During this time, Amitabh Bachchan was still emerging as a star and had just begun receiving appreciation from the public. He was very professional and punctual. The film fraternity respected and appreciated this immensely. Rajesh Khanna didn't react well to this and apparently said in an interview that he believed that clerks were punctual and that he was not a clerk, but an artist. Bragging about his position, he added that he was not a slave of his moods but instead, his moods were his slaves. Amitabh Bachchan, on hearing this, remained respectful to Rajesh Khanna.

Praising him, he admitted that Rajesh Khanna would always be the only superstar for him. He was highly impressed by the fact that the actor had appeared in 153 films by 1991, in a span of 25 years which included 101 solo and 21 multi-star-cast films. He was in awe of his immense hard work and respected that despite having three films releasing every year, he had managed to give 95 jubilee hits.

Following a Schedule

Despite his age and health issues, Amitabh Bachchan has remained disciplined with his gym regimen. He doesn't miss his exercise even for a day and in case he misses the regular morning hour, he compensates for the lost exercise at night before he goes to sleep. He hits the gym without fail at the break of dawn which keeps him rejuvenated for the rest of the day.

In an interview, he said, 'Bear it, struggle with it, allow it to tear into the body, scream out the music with effort and conclude with that something satisfaction of fighting an oddity.'

Amitabh Bachchan follows a strict schedule and firmly believes that life is a struggle. His father taught him this when he said, *'Jeevan ek sangharsh hai. Jab tak jeevan hai, tab tak sangharsh hai.'* (Life itself is a struggle. As long as there is life, there is struggle.)

He sometimes meets people as late as 11 p.m. at night to accommodate them and gives them all his attention. Most of us will suffer from a constant jet lag if we live like him. Even with such a hectic schedule, he manages to update his blog and Twitter to reach out to the world. In an interview with Ranbir Kapoor, he clarified that he didn't have a team to manage his Twitter and blog, and he did it all on his own.

'I never could have done what I have done without the habits of punctuality, order, and diligence, without the determination to concentrate myself on one subject at a time.'

—Charles Dickens

What can you learn from Amitabh on punctuality, responsiveness and promptness?

There are certain fundamentals that can deliver results when it comes to being punctual.

1. Discipline. Discipline. Discipline. There is no shortcut. If you want to be on time and manage your time well, you have to be a little harsh with yourself.
2. Be conscious about punctuality. Unless you make it your 'Key Result Area' or KRA, you will not be able to achieve anything.
3. Consider it good manners and proper grooming so that you don't look silly in front of others.
4. Plan your day in advance.
5. If you have an assistant, use that person upto the hilt to manage your schedules.
6. You can either use a dairy or an electronic gadget or even a mobile app—whatever suits you—to manage your time.
7. Carry forward your backlog to the next day if it is impossible to finish everything as planned.
8. Schedule time for interruptions and glitches. They do happen.
9. If you are getting late, you must inform the other person.
10. If you are late, apologize.
11. Make punctuality your trademark. People will love and respect you more.
12. Be polite to every one you deal with regardless of his / her status.
13. Always be prompt when responding to others' requests.

3

BOUNCING BACK AFTER FAILURE
When the Going Gets Tough, the Tough Get Going

'Courage is not having the strength to go on; it is going on when you don't have the strength.'

—Theodore Roosevelt

One of the most important traits of a strong person is the ability to take failures in his/her stride. Life is not always a bed of roses and there are good as well as bad phases which we all face during our lifetime. One has to be extremely fortunate to get success in the very first attempt and then to not face failure ever after that. Successful people in every field have faced failures at some point in their lives. Those who bounce back and try again are the ones who become successful.

If you look at well-known authors and their spectacular work, you would be surprised to discover that they managed success after many failures. J.K. Rowling, author of the popular *Harry Potter* series, had to face rejection from several publishing houses—almost a dozen—before her work was finally accepted. Rejections were not easy to accept as she was confident her work would appeal to the readers. She was also going through a financial crisis in her life at that time. Even when her manuscript was accepted, she was paid an advance of only GBP 1500 and 1000 copies were printed in the first go. Her fourth book was published some time later and it sold 372,775 copies in UK and more than three million copies in the US.

Today, 400 million copies of her books have been sold and she has an estimated wealth of GBP 600 million. Similarly, *Chicken Soup for the Soul* by Mark Victor Hansen and Jack Canfield was rejected 144 times before it was published. *Gone with the Wind* was also dismissed several times.

Soichiro Honda, the founder of Honda motor company, also had his share of failures. His factory where he made piston rings was bombed during World War II and later destroyed once again in an earthquake. But he didn't give up and instead used whatever raw material was available to him, including empty gasoline cans. He manufactured a tiny engine to fit on cycles to meet the increasing demand for cheap transport in those times. But soon, he faced financial difficulties and not knowing much about fiscal management, he asked his friend to join him. This is how he began making motorcycles and worked hard to construct the best bikes. In 1950, after his first motorcycle had been introduced in Japan, Honda stunned the engineering world by doubling the horsepower of the conventional four-stroke engine. With this technological innovation, the company was bound to be successful. By the end of the 1950s, Honda had won all the prestigious motorcycle racing prizes in the world and by 1954, it had achieved a 15 per cent share in the motorcycle market. This story shows how with determination, one can fight all odds and come out as a winner.

Life is a Struggle

> *'The man who moves a mountain begins by carrying away small stones.'*
>
> —Confucius

Once Amitabh Bachchan asked his father why one had to struggle so much in life. His father responded, *'Jeevan ek sangharsh hai. Jab tak jeevan hai, tab tak sangharsh hai.'* (Life itself is a struggle. As long as there is life, there is struggle.) Amitabh Bachchan, in an interview, recited a poem written by his father, Shri Harivansh Rai Bachchan. It speaks volumes about bouncing back after failure and the human struggle to survive.

'Nanhi cheenti jab dana lekar chadhti hai
Chadti deewaron paar sau baar girti hai
Chaad kaar girna gir kai chadna na usey akhardta hai
Aakhir uski mehanat bekar nahin hoti
Koshish karne walon ki kabhi haar nahin hoti.'

(The tiny ant, when it carries the grain
Lays it up into the heights of the wall
Falls slipping a hundred times,
Just as it tries again
The faith in the mind
Stirs courage in the nerves
It soars and slips, then slips and soars again
Until its efforts have not been in vain
The mind that dares
Has never been at loss.)

*'Many of life's failures are people who did not realize
how close they were to success when they gave up.'*

—Thomas A. Edison

The initial struggle to make a place for himself in the Indian film industry took Amitabh Bachchan almost four years during which he did small and insignificant roles. He thought of packing up his bags and going back several times but he held on each time and ended up staying. He made sure that he remained a part of the industry, no matter how small that part was. He improvised and made his voice his strength. Being flexible and open to small roles allowed him to remain relevant and stay connected with people from the industry and eventually, he did get his big break in Bollywood with *Anand*. 'Fortune favours the brave'—Amitabh Bachchan personifies this statement. He kept his hopes alive till he finally succeeded.

He once narrated a story. When he was young and staying with his father, he learnt an important lesson. One day, he saw his father moving a big and heavy boulder into their garden. It was impossible for someone to have carried such a heavy rock from across the road alone. He asked his father how he had managed to do it. His father told him that he had pushed it every day, moving it a few inches closer to their gate with every push. It had taken him several weeks to place it there.

A Fatal Accident

Sometimes life throws challenges for which one is not prepared. A similar thing happened with Amitabh Bachchan when he was on the sets of *Coolie.* He was shooting an action scene with Puneet Issar who was to hit him and Bachchan was to subsequently land on the table. During the fight sequence, he fell hard and was accidently injured by the corner of the table which caused a grievous internal damage. He went through an emergency surgery at a hospital in Bangalore and was later flown to Mumbai where he got treated at Breach Candy Hospital.

There was no sign of life in him for several days. He was almost in a comatose state. The entire nation prayed for him in temples and thronged the streets to the hospital to wish him good luck. His close friend, Rajiv Gandhi, called off his trip to the United States to be with him. It was a miraculous recovery for the actor and provided great relief to his family, friends and fans.

He revealed that he almost went into a coma-like situation

after the injury. Within five days of coming to Breach Candy, he had another surgery and didn't come out of that one for a very long time. He explained how he was clinically dead for a couple of minutes before Dr Wadia decided to take a last chance and began pumping cortisone injections into him one after another in the hope that something would happen. That is how he was revived.

While he was in the hospital, he had several tubes attached to his abdomen for treatment. When his children visited him, he bravely said, 'See, papa is flying kites!' Even in a crisis like that, he instructed his children to not miss school.

It took him several months to recover but as soon as he was back on his feet, he resumed work. He bounced back into action after a close shave with death. The movie *Coolie* was a super hit.

Politics and Downfall

> '*Success is not final, failure is not fatal: it is the courage to continue that counts.*'
>
> —Winston Churchill

In 1984, Amitabh Bachchan joined politics on Rajiv Gandhi's request. This was after the assassination of Indira Gandhi and Rajiv Gandhi required the support of the people he could count on. In such hard times, one needs people one can trust and Rajiv Gandhi trusted him completely. Amitabh won from the Allahabad constituency with a huge margin while Rajiv

Gandhi came back to power with majority. However, a few years later, the central government headed by Rajiv Gandhi as the prime minister of India was marred by the Bofor's scandal and Amitabh Bachchan also got entangled in it. He decided to quit and move back to the film industry. Though he came out clean from the Bofor's scandal, he was emotionally very hurt.

His movies thereafter didn't do too well. The movie *Shahenshah* did reasonably well but was not good enough to reinstate him as the 'shahenshah' (emperor) of Bollywood. The times and moods were changing and the audience was looking for something different. They were not ready to accept old predictable stories that had entertained them a decade ago.

Movies like *Agneepath* demonstrated his great dialogue delivery and acting prowess but failed to get him on the top again. It was forced retirement for him. He was no more a dependable entity for the film fraternity. Film industry can be very harsh when one's time is up. The same happened to him—he was written off.

Amitabh Bachchan Corporation Limited (ABCL) Fiasco and How He Got Out of It

Not getting success is one thing but achieving success and losing everything is more destructive to the body, mind and soul. Amitabh Bachchan managed to succeed against all odds after a struggle of almost four years. Post the raging success of *Zanjeer* in 1973; he achieved the stardom that thousands aspired for. He remained the undisputed superstar of Indian cinema for more than two decades. However, misfortune struck once again. Failure in the public glare can be devastating. It is the psychological impact that takes its toll in such cases and it is hard to overcome. Your failure is seen and scrutinized by those who once adored you. That is exactly what happened to him.

This was the time when Amitabh Bachchan ventured into business with the launch of ABCL in 1995. The vision was to build a mega entertainment company which would bring everything connected to the entertainment industry under one roof. It included producing and distributing films, selling music rights, TV production and event management. The group moved pretty fast and recruited 150 top professionals from different fields. It launched 15 films and dabbled in music rights of several others. The initial start was encouraging as the company managed its target turnover of 65 crores, registering a profit of 15 crores. The second year was when the problems started. Amitabh Bachchan agreed to do shows abroad but did not route the billing through ABCL. The senior team didn't appreciate this and finally, the top management was fired and a new team moved in. Sanjay Gupta, the CEO was replaced by Gautam Berry. But things didn't change. Moreover, their own production *Mrityudaata* did poorly at the box office.

The Miss World beauty pageant was the last straw. A British company made an offer to ABCL to handle the contest in India for them. They wanted to shift the venue from Sun City to India and were looking for an Indian company to sponsor it. They had four months to get going and host the event. Amitabh Bachchan was sceptical as he felt the time was less. As the captain of the ship, he asked his crew i.e. the ABCL professional team if they would be able to deliver. The team was gung-ho and confident they would pull it off.

Hence, the prestigious pageant took place in Bangalore on 23 November 1996. Eighty-eight contestants took part and it was successfully concluded. There were protests by women's groups but it was finally conducted without any big hitch. The aftermath, however, was financially backbreaking as the contestant who won the pageant demanded a fee of $2 million and combined with other costs, the bill ended up being $5 million. It was a financial fiasco.

A BBC online poll conducted in 1999 named Amitabh Bachchan the 'Superstar of the Millennium', over the likes of Alec Guinness and Marlon Brando of Hollywood. But at the same time, the situation at ABCL was very bad. The public confidence had taken a nosedive and salaries were not being paid as money was stuck in the production and distribution of films. Amitabh Bachchan was being hounded by creditors. He was shocked to see that the same people who had treated him with so much respect and awe a few months back started being rude and discourteous. It was very demeaning for him.

In June 2000, he became the first living Asian to have a wax statue curetted in his honour at Madame Tussauds. However, the same year brought a tsunami of financial and emotional troubles for him. When the entire world was busy celebrating the new century, Amitabh Bachchan was cursing his disastrous fortune. He had no films, no money, no company and a million legal cases against him. The tax authorities had even put a notice of recovery on his house. In one of his interviews, he admitted that he had very little knowledge of managing finance and business and went along with whatever his top management advised him to do. That was a big mistake.

In a TV interview, when he was asked if he had any regrets that the film industry and the professional fraternity didn't come to his rescue during his difficult times, he responded candidly by declaring that it was his decision and he had not expected someone else to take that responsibility and help him. He added that he had no regrets and didn't hold anyone responsible.

The Indian Board for Industrial and Financial Reconstruction declared Amitabh Bachchan Corporation Limited a 'sick' company with a debt of $ 14 million. His friends advised them to close the losing venture and move on but they decided to clear all their debts despite huge losses. They re-started the production of films.

Amitabh Bachchan clawed his way back from the abyss of gloom. Slowly and gradually, he began returning the 90 crores he owed to different people. Remembering those days, he told *India Today* that he paid one and all, including Doordarshan. When they asked for the interest component, he did commercials for them. He revealed he could never forget how creditors used to land at his door, be abusive, threaten and demand, and worse still, when they came for '*kudkee*' at Prateeksha, his residence. These were difficult times for Bachchan, not just financially, but emotionally too. After all, here was the presiding deity of Indian cinema, virtually bankrupt.

He added that there was a sword hanging on his head all the time and that he spent many sleepless nights. He had no films. His house and a small property in New Delhi were attached. He felt like everything was going wrong together. He also admitted that it was without a doubt one of the darkest moments in his 44-year-old professional career. It made him sit and think, and look for options and different scenarios. The answer came to him one day and he walked to Yash Chopra who stayed behind his house. He implored him to give him work. That is how he got *Mohabbatein*.

The megastar fought back with honesty and humility even if that meant going and requesting a producer to give him work. You need strength of character and resilience to undergo such pressure and be ready to do whatever it takes—even bending backwards—to remain afloat. After he was offered a role in *Mohabbatein* by Yash Chopra on his request, he started doing commercials, television shows and films. And today, he has managed to repay his entire debt of 90 crores and has started afresh.

While conquering failure, ethics also played a huge role for him. It would have been easier for him to declare himself bankrupt and take a softer option. Yet, he demonstrated grace under tremendous pressure. He exhibited honesty and refused to move on with a blot on his name. Very few would have done what he did in this situation.

'Perseverance is the hard work you do after you get tired of doing the hard work you already did.'

—Newt Gingrich

What can you learn from Amitabh on resilience and honour?

1. Accept defeat as a part of your destiny but never feel that you have been defeated.
2. Experimenting with life is something which one must always do.
3. Despite physical disabilities, your determination can take you forward.
4. Strong and ethical people fight it out and emerge as winners.
5. Don't blame others for your failures and wrong decisions.
6. Identify what you are good at and use that strength to bounce back.
7. Demonstrate grace under pressure.
8. Help friends who need you in crisis.
9. Be honest and return people's money, come what may. Don't take shortcuts or bend rules to protect yourself.
10. Don't betray the trust of people who invested in you and your reputation.
11. If you are genuine and honest, God and destiny will also support you.
12. Prayers of people seldom go waste.
13. Earning goodwill is more important than earning money.

4

APPRECIATING OTHERS
Humility, Cooperation and Diplomacy

'Appreciation is a wonderful thing: It makes what is excellent in others belong to us as well.'

—Voltaire

Appreciating Others and Humility are the Greatest Human Traits

People who appreciate their colleagues, friends and family are always held in high esteem by others. If an accomplished personality does this, he is admired for being down to earth and someone who does not demonstrate ego. Appreciation is a very important part of human competence within the realms of Emotional Intelligence. Most of us either forget to appreciate others or do not feel the need to do so. In a structured organization like a corporation, the boundaries are well-defined. You know who the boss is and who the subordinate is. Good leaders and bosses appreciate their teammates to keep the team's morale high.

Showbiz, however, is highly ego driven. In an organized sector, if you are no longer in the good books of your boss, you have a choice of leaving the organization and making a living elsewhere. But life in film industry is as Raj Kapoor said in his film *Mera Naam Joker* (1970), '*Jeena Yahan Marna Yahan, Iske Siwa Jaana Kahan.*' (We have to live our life here and also die here, where else can one go?) In Bollywood, you have fewer options. If you fall, you drop with a thud. The entire industry dismisses you, the audience rejects you—it is ruthless. Yet, if you appreciate others in this ego driven environment, your colleagues and people remember you for your good temperament.

In a profession like the show business where the lines are either not defined or are pretty blurred at best, it is difficult to decide who stands where. Seniority is not defined by the years an actor or a director has been in the business. It is also difficult to decide who is at the top in terms of popularity and affection of the audience. Having said that, there are always undisputed legends who command a different level of respect from the audience as well as their co-workers. They are labelled with the help of loosely defined lexicons such as megastars, superstars, King of Bollywood or even Badshah.

Amitabh Bachchan is one such personality who commands admiration from every single person irrespective of the situation. The only actor to be called 'one man industry', he has been on the pedestal for decades now, notwithstanding his ups and downs. The man has earned great respect within the film fraternity. Another reason for that is his habit of praising people who deserve to be praised. A good upbringing, level-headedness and a bit of diplomacy is appreciated and noticed by others and it works in the long run.

Humility

Humility earns you the respect of others more than anything else. Mr Bachchan charmed the contestants of *KBC* by treating every contestant and their family with dignity and respect. He would impress them in every episode. The logic is simple: if you respect others, others will respect you.

Appreciation for His Co-stars

When Amitabh Bachchan was struggling to be noticed, Rajesh Khanna was already a superstar. But later, in a way, he replaced Rajesh Khanna. In an interview, however, Bachchan confessed that he had never expected to play lead roles. He always thought he was not conventionally good-looking and felt that he would never look as good as Rajesh Khanna. He revealed that once when he had seen a photograph of Rajesh Khanna in Filmfare, he had thought, '*Yaar, ye aadmi kya khaata hai*? *Iske gaal itne lal kaise hain*?' (What does this man eat? How are his cheeks so red?)

In a rare interview, Amitabh Bachchan clarified that whether it was on the sets of *Anand* or *Namak Haraam*, Rajesh Khanna and him never bickered, argued or tried to upstage one another in any manner. On the contrary, when he was working in Calcutta and was keen to join films, his inspiration was Mr Khanna. He recalled how happy he had been when Hrishikesh Mukherjee asked him to work with Rajesh Khanna in *Anand*. It was a dream come true for him. He mentioned modestly that he got famous purely because he was working with Khanna. People came and asked him questions like 'How does he look?' and 'What does he do?' He has always had the greatest respect for Rajesh Khanna.

Accepting the same, Rajesh Khanna admitted that when he saw *Namak Haraam* at a trial at Liberty cinema, he knew his time was up. 'Here is the superstar of tomorrow,' he had told Hrishikesh Mukherjee.

Reflecting on the younger film actors, he is of the opinion that one needs to give them more time. He has maintained that it is a little harsh to put them aside as they are working in a much more competitive climate than the actors before them. The audiences too, are not as tolerant as they were before. He admitted that the audience gave him a lot of breathing space and allowed him to make mistakes and rectify them film after film. But now it was the turn of the younger actors because today's audience lay between 18 and 30. He narrated an incident to prove his point. When he was shooting with Govinda for *Hum,* a group of young kids came up to him asking for an autograph. Govinda was standing next to him. There was a young cute girl who poked him and said, '*Woh nahin, ye. Govinda ka autograph lo.*' (Not him, but this guy. Take Govinda's autograph.)

> *'The deepest craving of human nature*
> *is the need to be appreciated.'*

—William James

In an interview with Ranbir Kapoor where he praised his work immensely, Bachchan admitted that he could hardly dance and in fact hated it. He thought it was incredible that people could move different parts of their bodies in different directions with such ease.

He is all praises for the youngsters of today, always encouraging them to do better. He has mentioned on various occasions that professionally, he is fond of Deepika Padukone. He admires her work, ethics, composure and determined efforts to improve. She was on cloud nine when he sent her a handwritten note. The note appreciated her efforts and congratulated her for her performance in *Goliyon Ki Rasleela Ram-Leela* (2013).

In an interview, Deepika revealed that she would cherish it forever. She didn't get into the details but she was highly appreciative of the gesture as people don't often send a handwritten note and a huge bouquet of flowers nowadays. Richa Chaddha who played Deepika's sister-in-law in the film *Ram-Leela* also received a note from Big B. Richa was overjoyed and admitted that it was a huge deal to receive it from him.

He is full of appreciation for the upcoming actors and from a legend like him; the praises can be highly motivating. All those who do well in life and are in some position of power must do this. I, as the director of a management institute, started a 'Directors Debut Award' for the most promising student of the incoming batch. This became such a sought-after award that the first year students worked very hard to get it. It encouraged them to excel. I also started giving books as prizes to the topper of each subject. There could be only one topper in a class but there were a dozen toppers in total, one in each subject! This made for a number of heroes every semester and was a big morale booster.

Rajnikanth and Big B started their careers in 1970 but Amitabh has been extremely appreciative of Rajnikanth as well. In a recent interview, he was quoted praising him. He said that Rajnikanth was phenomenal—the largest, the best and truly the boss of Indian cinema. He added that he was terrific company on the sets and a fine gentleman. He admitted that they were friends and even made an exception for him by labelling him with an epithet—a practice he usually abhors. He praised Rajnikanth's hard work, talent and belief and admired his determination that had raised him to this stature. Despite his extraordinary career and incomparable adulation, he was a simple and down-to-earth person and that is something Big B appreciates a lot. He even revealed that a Fiat car Rajnikanth had bought when he had attained his early success remained with him till recently, providing an evidence of his simplicity.

For Amitabh Bachchan, Dilip Kumar has been his idol and an actor who gave something new to every take he shot. He also added that he appreciated every performance of Waheeda Rehman and considered her a true Indian beauty. For him, she was the ultimate personification of the Indian woman. Apart from the grace of her presence, he always found her mischievous quality most endearing. Al Pacino and Marlon

Brando are his all-time favourite Hollywood actors and he immensely appreciates their performances as well.

'Saying thank you is more than good manners. It is good spirituality.'

—Alfred Painter

Though one cannot downplay the importance of story, script and dialogue writing, the director is the captain of the ship in the film industry. Big B is a director's actor. He believes that a film is a director's vision and an actor must help him achieve that. He might give suggestions but if the director wants something, he does it without an argument. He has worked with almost every director in the film industry and has always been appreciative of them. This shows his humility. Instead of taking all the credit for himself, he believes in the value of teamwork.

When talking about directors, it was Hrishikesh Mukherjee who gave Amitabh his first significant role, casting him with Rajesh Khanna. While people looked at Amitabh Bachchan as an angry, young and a tough guy, Mukherjee noticed his softer side. He extracted something different from the actor in every film—humour, comedy, sadness, angst and even jealousy. They did nine films together and Amitabh gave some of his most memorable performances in *Anand*, *Abhimaan*, *Guddi* and *Chupke Chupke*. True as an actor, he never allowed his personality to overshadow the characters he played in Hrishida's films which depicted everyday life.

Amitabh admitted that the director knew how to say

the 'simplest of the stories' in the most exciting manner and praised his exceptional sense of budget. While remembering late Hrishikesh Mukherjee on his birth anniversary, he wrote in his blog that when Jaya Bhaduri and he decided to get married; Hrishikesh Mukherjee was the first person after their parents whom they informed, along with Khwaja Ahmad Abbas, his first film director.

Big B cannot forget the time when he had met the icon on his hospital bed towards the end. He recalled in his blog how during Hrishikesh Mukherjee's last days when he was in the ICU (Intensive Care Unit), his entire body was riddled with tubes and wires. His eyes were shut and the ventilator was helping his body breathe. Bachchan remembered how Hrishida had suddenly woken up and his face had brightened as soon as he had seen him. Through all the tapes, bottles and wires, his eyes had beckoned him to come closer. And then, with great effort, he had pulled out his hand and put it on Bachchan's head, asking him to leave. The next day he had passed away.

Another director Amitabh Bachchan owes his box office successes to is Manmohan Desai. He had the ability to extract the best out of him, just like Hrishikesh Mukherjee. They pulled off greats like *Mard* (1985), *Coolie, Naseeb* (1981) and *Parvarish* (1977). They gave their best together in *Amar Akbar Anthony* (1977).

Bachchan mentioned in an interview how on the first day of his first film with Manmohan Desai, his remark was clean, crisp and conclusive. Bachchan had attempted to explain himself but it had not been entertained. It was the last time he had ever disagreed with him. In their long association that followed over 20 glorious years after that, there was never a doubt about who the master was.

He added that it was the strength of his conviction that prevented one from arguing over an illogical situation with him. To him, it was the cinema that was important—the cinema which in his own words was 'not going to be seen at the Cannes Film Festival, but at Chinchpokli.'

Bachchan, who endearingly addressed Manmohan Desai as Manji, said that though he was a simple man, his imagination was far removed from simplicity. It touched the unbelievable, leaving those who worked with him and the millions who saw his creation speechless and gasping for breath. His elation at the time of the conception of his films seemed to naturally flow into his actors, writers and technicians, so that by the time the product reached the masses it was impossible for them to not be entirely consumed by the heady potent mixture. He had the ability to entice the audience into the theatre and once they were securely in their seats, he would nail them there. Bachchan revealed that Manji absolutely abhorred the idea of going to see his own film in a theatre because he could not tolerate seeing anyone get up from their place. He narrated how on one occasion he even pulled a person back to his chair!

According to Big B, he was a meticulous planner. Be it the timing of a shooting shift two years down the line or the security arrangements for his son Ketan's wedding, he would go about it personally with the astuteness and thoroughness of an army general.

He revealed that when he had to be shifted in a critical

condition from Bangalore to Bombay after his accident on the sets of *Coolie*, Manji actually ran with the ambulance from the hospital to the airport to assure that he had a comfortable ride and an appropriate route was taken in order to avoid the potholes.

> *'If you want to turn your life around, try thankfulness.*
> *It will change your life mightily.'*
>
> —Gerald Good

About his craft, Bachchan said that there was a certain brashness in his presentations. Whether it was his leading man emerging from an Easter egg or his hero wooing his opposite number on a kabaddi pitch, it was done with panache. One knew that they were being taken for a ride, but they went for it anyway.

Remembering Yash Chopra and Hrishikesh Mukherjee, Bachchan revealed that he was a romantic by heart; he was fond of poetry in everything. He added that Yashji was someone who shot *Deewaar* and *Kabhi Kabhie* simultaneously—subjects that were worlds apart. On the other hand, assistant to the great Bimal Roy, Hrishida's subjects were powerful, real, middle of the path and successful.

He has great admiration for the way he rose from a small office to an empire because of sheer hard work and talent. He still remembers what Yash Chopra said on his birthday and confessed that his words still rung in his ears and what remained was the resonance of his goodness and feelings. Apart from his praises for his work, what he liked most about

Bachchan was that he had been a good son and above all, a good human being.

Talking about Prakash Mehra of *Zanjeer*, he said that Prakashji was a great storyteller. The way he narrated his story, he never bothered about camera angles. He just put the camera in one place and told the actors *'chalo start karo'* (Come on, begin). On the other hand, Manmohan Desai was completely different. He had to have massive sets, just the grandeur of everything was more important to him.

Remembering his most memorable performance in *Black* which won him a Filmfare Award, Bachchan praised Sanjay Leela Bhansali by saying that the craft of the young and dynamic director and the freedom he allowed his actors helped him carve out his own interpretation of the role he was playing. Barring one mistake that he made in the performance which he believed was his own personal failing; he admitted that Sanjay Leela Bhansali presented all his actors in such wondrous roles that it was sheer joy to see the final product on screen. A film made by Bhansali is one big painting for Bachchan.

Amitabh Bachchan is not just full of good words for everyone; he also remembers the words of appreciation that were spoken for him. He remembered Dilip Kumar's praises after watching *Black*. Dilip Kumar was moved but it was Bachchan who was in tears when he saw him standing outside the theatre waiting to greet him after the film was over. He just held his hands and said nothing. That moment conveyed everything to Big B.

*'To get the full value of joy you must have
someone to divide it with.'*

—Mark Twain

New-age directors have cast Big B in different roles with every single movie. And for that too, he has been ever thankful. He is full of admiration for the new directors of the industry. He is impressed by the immense talent they possess. Bachchan has always marvelled at the sheer perfection in their very first outing. He mentioned how he could never find any mistakes and that he loved seeing them approach their work in such a relaxed way.

From his directorial debut film, *Cheeni Kum* to *Shamitabh* (2015), R. Balki has cast Bachchan in quirky and unusual roles. Both appreciate and respect each other immensely. Shoojit Sircar and Big B have come up with some critically acclaimed films as well.

Shoojit described their experience together. He said that with Mr Bachchan, their film journey began with the shooting of *Shoebite* (2019) and their association has been strong even after 10 years. He mentioned that it was purely a working relationship in the beginning, and then, they became friends. The trust developed between the two and they bonded. Even for *Pink*, when Shoojit approached Bachchan, he agreed to do the film immediately. Balki acknowledged the fact that Bachchan trusted him a lot even when he was coming with a new director like Aniruddha Roy Chowdhury.

As an actor, Mr Bachchan said that Shoojit often put him in challenging environments and convinced him that just because he was old, it did not necessarily give him the ability or the acumen to play old in front of the camera. Many times, Shoojit told him how to enact a particular scene.

Amitabh Bachchan has worked with a host of Bengali film-makers in his career and the actor maintains that it is a privilege to work with them because they have an ability to touch a certain nerve. From Mirnal Sen, Hrishida, Shakti Samanta, Pramod Chakravorty, Dulal Guha, Basu Chatterjee and Shoojit, he believes that it is a blessing that they have chosen him for various films in the past as according to him, Bengali directors have a certain sensibility.

Big B even notices the new-age critics. Praising bloggers, he said that some of their remarks are always well-written beyond comprehension. He is highly impressed with the way they look at a film and give criticism and he said in an interview that their assessment on why a film did well and what one should have done to make it work is usually brilliant.

Praising People Who May Not Matter

This is one trait which most of us do not have and it is almost non-existent in a glamour-driven industry. Why should a megastar bother to think about people who work as stuntmen, extras, body doubles and junior artists?

Great people, however, try to ensure that they step down from their high pedestal and encourage those who are involved in the background, making them look larger than life. They understand the importance of making others feel special because of the work they do. It is not everyone who realizes that every type of work is essential and of consequence when it comes to the complete picture. Amitabh Bachchan never loses an opportunity to publically praise the people—men and women who give their best years to make this industry tick and transform megastars from the ordinary mortals they actually are. He also realizes that every star has his days and a day of oblivion will strike each one however big that person may be at the present moment.

In one of his interviews, he said that it is always painful to see some of the highly successful stars of yesteryears struggling to survive when no one bothers for them. He recalled how once he had seen an old person waiting for a bus and had recognized him instantly as a man of reckoning in the film industry a few decades ago. He was in his car and had gone to offer him a lift. But that person was so embarrassed that Bachchan had recognized him, he had said, 'Thank you, I will take the bus but don't tell anyone that you saw me in this condition.'

If each one of us realizes that success won't last forever and that the power we have today may disappear soon; it will help us in being grounded and humane. The same thing is true for appreciation. If you respect people on your way up, they will respect you when you are on your way to the bottom.

> *'Gratitude is not only the greatest of virtues,*
> *but the parent of all others.'*
>
> —Marcus Tullius Cicero

What can you learn from Amitabh on the art of appreciating others?

1. Appreciation does not cost money but it helps to build a great reputation.
2. If you respect others, others will respect you.
3. Whatever stature you acquire, a drop of appreciation for colleagues can act like an ocean of potent potion.
4. You must give credit to those who have helped you in your career. Don't ever forget them.
5. The higher you go, your appreciation carries more weight and people value it. So use it more often.
6. People may not remember you for anything else but they will always remember you for your kind words.
7. Appreciation is the quality of kings. If you think you are a king, be generous with your words for others.
8. Don't praise only those who matter. It is a sign of greatness to be appreciative of those who don't matter—after all, they are human beings too. Their blessings will go a long way.
9. If a megastar like Amitabh Bachchan can be courteous and can appreciate his colleagues, then each one of us can learn to do that from him.
10. If you appreciate others, others will appreciate you. Period.

5

HANDLING HEALTH ISSUES WITH YOUR CHIN UP

Managing the Unmanageable

'No one saves us but ourselves. No one can and no one may. We ourselves must walk the path.'

—Buddha

Mild fever, toothache, upset stomach, running nose or a sore throat can take a toll on our daily chores. Some of us have to even miss examinations or skip important meetings because of these issues. It is difficult to be yourself when you have a splitting headache or a sprain in the back. We are unable to perform our duties effectively due to such minor illnesses. In such situations, one is often in a bad mood, unable to concentrate or even sit through a presentation in the office.

Most of us in the 'urban professions' have a set routine, a reasonably comfortable working environment and work ethics that permit us to take it easy if one is under the weather. Actors live a very different life. They have unruly working schedules often disrupted by factors beyond anyone's control. They sometimes have to work under harsh conditions for hours together. Studios are hot and humid, and blazing lights, painted sets and light reflectors add to the discomfort. Dance sequences have blaring music and not a very comfortable setup to work in. Though film-makers try their best to keep the actors comfortable, they cannot do anything after a point due to natural constraints which have to be accepted as hazards of the profession.

If donning make-up, using a wig or moustache or wearing heavy unwieldy costumes is not enough, the noises on sets make it worse. Film actors invariably have to shoot outdoors for some portions of the movie. It could be freezing cold if one shoots in a hill station or extremely hot if the shooting takes place in a desert during summers. Jungles could be hot and humid. There can be artificial breeze created with blowers and huge fans or a downpour using big showers from top can be involved in the scene. One could be drenched for hours in an uncomfortable outfit. Action sequences can often get tiring and sometimes even injurious to health. On top of it, one has to act according to the script and the dictates of the director, shot after shot. Whatever gets captured in these uneasy circumstances remain in the movie. This is the performance which remains for people to judge forever. Actors, therefore, cannot take it easy. They have to put their best foot forward at all times.

Amitabh Bachchan has been in the film industry for more than four decades and has done it all—fight sequences, songs and dances, action-packed performances, emotional drama and great dialogue delivery. He has often performed in the harshest of conditions but regardless of the circumstances, his performances have been more than perfect, without a blemish or even a shade of mediocrity.

Unfortunately, he has been on the wrong side of good health for most of his acting career. It was not mild cold, headache or a toothache. He had more serious issues which continue to trouble and haunt him till date. Most of us would simply give up in the face of so much agony but he didn't.

'Health is relative. There is no such thing as an absolute state of health or sickness. Everyone's physical, mental, and emotional condition is a combination of both.'

—Theodore Isaac Rubin

The first time he went under the knife was much before he joined the film industry. When he was a student in Delhi University, a lump was noticed on the left side of his neck. He was operated twice but the lump was not removed as it was benign and located very deep under the nerves. In Calcutta, he was operated by a doctor who said he would remove the lump as it wasn't pleasant to look at. He did remove the lump but accidently, he also cut a nerve that held the shoulder muscle. That is why his left shoulder droops a bit.

He has revealed that it is not a style. He does not have the muscle, so it droops. Therefore, it is difficult for him to raise his left arm and the misfortune is that he is a lefty. If he does raise it, it drops immediately because it has no strength of its own. When he eats, he needs to rest his arm on the table for support otherwise he cannot lift it up to his mouth. His shoulder and neck pain that he has often talked of is not because of strain, but because of the remaining working muscle on his shoulder compensating for the loss of the muscle on the other side.

He added that not having even 20 per cent strength in his left hand which is his more powerful hand purely because of the surgical accident is a huge handicap.

Amitabh Bachchan went through his second health problem when he was injured on the sets of *Coolie*. He was operated in Bangalore and later in Mumbai. These were major surgeries which left him weak and took several months to recover. During these surgeries in 1982, several holes were made in his abdomen and rubber strips were used to remove impurities from the stomach. Even after their removal, the scars remained forever. He jokingly once said that there was a mini golf course on his stomach as there were 18 holes which had left permanent marks.

He wrote in his blog that once the stomach muscle is cut, it never gets back to its original strength. And since all body action, at least all the vital ones are controlled by the stomach muscle, his actions or the ability to execute them diminished considerably.

A few years later, he went through a third stomach surgery because of an unexplainable pain in his stomach. Several stomach operations had led to hernia in his lower abdomen, causing severe pain when he stood for too long or walked for a while. His ability to run, get up quickly and jump was compromised majorly. He admitted that during dance and action scenes, there was an intense pain and he usually countered that with a hernia belt which was temporary and not really a cure. That was when he decided to get the surgery done. Mr Bachchan is also asthmatic and has to carry an asthma pump with him all the time. This surely causes an impediment in his action sequences and sometimes, even in his dialogue delivery.

'People think celebrities don't have to worry about human things like sickness and death and rent. It's like you've traveled to this Land of Celebrity, this other country. They want you to tell about what you saw.'

—David Duchovny

Almost a year after the *Coolie* accident in 1982, he was struck with another health issue. While climbing up the steps of a hotel where he was shooting for one of Manmohan Desai's films, he suddenly fell down from the stairs. He described the sensation in his blog and said that he could not even raise his arms or walk more than a few steps. He was unable to brush his teeth, drink water or purse his lips. They rushed him back to Breach Candy Hospital in Mumbai and he was diagnosed with myasthenia gravis, a muscle dysfunctional disorder. He explained that the situation was so bad that if his eyes shut, they would not open on their own and if they opened, they did not close without help. He had to use toothpicks to open them. Treatment started with mestinon, a tablet that would get him functional and he would slip back into listlessness as soon as the effect wore off. Eight to ten tablets a day kept him going. He was told that it was dormant but could resurface anytime.

As if his troubles were not enough, a firecracker (anaar) exploded in his left hand a year later on Diwali. The skin of his hand melted below his wrist and his left hand became a pulp, with no nails and fingers. He could not be given general anaesthesia as he had been given enough during his earlier surgeries. Mr Bachchan insisted on local anaesthesia which naturally made it an extremely painful ordeal. His movie *Inquilaab* (1984) was on the floors and he had to shoot it in Chennai. Doctors told him that it was too soon but he wanted to keep his commitment and reported for the shooting with a bandaged hand.

> *'It's a war zone, my body, and one which has been through a great deal.'*
>
> —Amitabh Bachchan

He revealed that the skin was so raw that even a gust of breeze on it would make him wince in pain. His fingers and palm gradually began to come back along with the nails, but they were still unusable because they had lost all strength and could not be moved. Another film *Sharaabi* (1984) was scheduled for shooting. As an actor, he was not sure how he would do it. Therefore, throughout the shooting, he kept his left hand in the pocket. He revealed that during a song sequence, he was to hit the 'ghungroo' and he used his left hand which began bleeding. It hurt tremendously but he proceeded to shoot the scene despite severe pain. He stated frankly that a kind of madness took over him as an actor when the camera started rolling. It took him weeks to get his thumb to move across and touch his index finger. It took many months before all his fingers got mobile and operational and many years before all the burn scars dissolved.

> 'Hope doesn't require a massive chain where heavy links of logic hold it together. A thin wire will do... just strong enough to get us through the night until the winds die down.'

> —Charles R. Swindoll

But it wasn't over yet. Another health bomb was waiting to explode. In a routine check-up by his family doctor, it was discovered that 75 per cent of his liver had failed due to cirrhosis which he had contracted by the blood donated to him during his operations in 1982. It had come from several donors and probably one of them had been infected. Only 25 per cent of his liver was functioning. During this ordeal, a lump was also discovered in the groin region and was cut under local anaesthesia. It was then sent for biopsy as they suspected cancer. It took 10 days for the result to come and he was then shooting daily for *KBC*. He was worried as anyone would be, yet he turned up every day for the shooting with a smile on his face and a bounce in his gait. He confessed that those 10 days were like waiting for the guillotine.

One wonders what kind of strength can lead to such perseverance and determination in the face of trouble. He was not sure what would happen and if it had turned out to be cancer, the only treatment would have been chemotherapy which would disfigure his face and turn him very weak. But he kept going and after 10 days when the results were negative, he jumped with joy. Despite the immense tension and anxiety in those trying days, he gave great performances, keeping his emotions under check. He must be made of steel to pull this off with such grace.

This joy did not last long because he was soon detected with tuberculosis of the spine. It wasn't a complete surprise as he had been complaining of severe backache for a while.

He said in a matter-of-fact way that he was experiencing severe spinal pains and he was under the impression that the KBC chair was the cause of it. So he started popping painkillers to get him through the episodes on TV—eight to ten every day.

To top it all, he as an actor has done thousands of action sequences which have injured his legs and have caused circulation problems. During the shooting of *Don* and *Parvarish*, it was discovered that his L4 and L5 vertebrae were damaged in the lower spine. Though doctors suggested surgery, he refused as he had had enough of them. An American doctor in New York, where he had gone for an opinion on his myasthenia, wanted to see his medical report. Bachchan recalled that when the doctor had gone through his report, he had inquired, 'Is this guy still alive? I cannot suggest anything more than what he has already been treated for but I would just like to meet the man.'

It is clear that the man has gone through troubled times with many ailments hammering him one after the other. If one has to summarize his health issues, he is asthmatic, has had three major stomach surgeries, suffered tuberculosis of the spine, lost most of his shoulder muscle in an operation, lost almost 80 per cent of its strength, has problems with hernia, suffered myasthenia gravis, lost 75 per cent of his liver to hepatitis, had several vertebra damaged due to action sequences and injury in the neck, and has also met with an accident which burnt his hand to a pulp. Needless to say, all these health issues have caused him tremendous pain, physical discomfort and mental agony. Can anyone go through more discomfort than this?

Despite this, he is still on his feet every single day. Daily hitting the gym, shooting for films and actively participating in functions on a regular basis is something which seems impossible for a 75-year old man with the kind of medical history he has. Most of his ailments still exist and many of them are troublesome, painful and exhausting. Medicines, a controlled diet and severe restrictions for survival can hit anyone emotionally. But this man is different.

It is simply incredible to see him perform day after day in front of the camera, giving his best every single time. The man doesn't tire. He doesn't give up. And he definitely doesn't give any excuses. There is no sign of discomfort or pain on his face. He follows a punishing schedule. He has seen the worst of times in his life but he never complains in public, is always on time and is great with words and gracious in behaviour.

This kind of strength is not usually seen in ordinary mortals. He is a man for all seasons and someone who takes the punch straight on the chin and still keeps it high up.

'You gain strength, courage, and confidence by every experience in which you really stop to look fear in the face. You are able to say to yourself, "I lived through this horror. I can take the next thing that comes along." You must do the thing you think you cannot do.'

—Eleanor Roosevelt

What can you learn from Amitabh about never giving up in life?

1. We all have our share of illnesses but it is up to us how we take it in our stride.
2. Do not use minor health-related problems as excuses to not do your duty. There are people with much bigger health issues who take these as a part of their lives and move on every single day.
3. If you want to stick to your commitment, sickness must not slow you down.
4. Life is not a bed of roses for the rich and famous. Some of them just make it look like that.
5. If Amitabh Bachchan can do it, you can surely try.
6. If you are mentally strong and committed to your work, you can overcome any obstacle—however difficult it may be.

6

OLD VALUES, MODERN OUTLOOK

Respect, Integrity, Values and Philanthropy

'Work doesn't tire you...the audience that waits does.
They give courage and command and direction... We glow
in their love.'

—Amitabh Bachchan

If one has to simplify Emotional intelligence, one can perceive it as a distilled form of age-old values which many consider to be outdated. Unfortunately, that is the biggest misnomer.

While Gautama Buddha talked of vipassana leading to an equanimous mind around 600 BC, Aristotle was dealing with anger management around 300 BC. We all have been grappling with these problems for the past centuries. Great theories of mind and matter emerged 2000 to 3000 years ago. Hindu Shastras and Upanishads taught us these values and they have remained with us till date. They taught us to live our lives in a more holistic and dignified way. If caring for people and love was important a thousand years ago, it is important even today. If dishonesty was wrong in the last century, it is wrong even now. People continue to respect commitment today also. These simple ethics are important for any and every profession. Value-based living can never become outdated.

Albert Einstein who taught at Princeton University asked one question in the final paper year after year. He was once asked by a student, 'Sir, I notice that one question is repeated in every final examination paper you set. Don't you think it is very easy for students to answer this question?' Einstein replied, 'My friend, the question remains the same but the answer changes every year.' He explained that theories in science change as we discover new things. Our understanding improves as we move along.

In case of human values, problem changes year after year, but the answer always remains the same—stick to your basic values. Problems faced by our parents were different than what we faced in our youth. Therefore, every generation faces different challenges but the solution lies in following the age-old principles. These values will always act as anchors in our troubled times.

Modern studies carried out more scientifically also point out that great leaders and great people owed their success more to these values than their professional acumen. Leaders of nations, corporate honchos, researchers, academicians and creative people who did well had their value systems in place.

We need to teach these values to ourselves and to our children even more vigorously. Having been surrounded by young men and women as a teacher for over two decades, I am a firm believer of the fact that these values cannot be taught without actually practising them. We need to identify the great icons of excellence as role models of value based living. Amitabh Bachchan is one such person who demonstrates integrity, chivalry and what we call good 'sanskars'.

> *'My father was very energetic; my mother was very energetic. He lived to a very old age, and so did my mother. I believe that I just have it from my father, from my parents. They had wonderful energy.'*

—Donald Trump

Respecting and Looking After Your Parents

Respecting one's parents is becoming old-fashioned now. Rebelling against elders is the new fashion mantra. 'I will do it my way. Who are you to tell me what is right or wrong?' is the trending statement. We do less work but fight more for freedom of speech, expression, dressing up the way we want and the freedom to eat and drink what we like. We feel proud to rebel. We all are running fast but we don't know where to. The modern generation is neither prepared to look after their parents nor do they find time for their kids who are best looked after in day care facilities. Imagine leaving your 80-year-old mother in an old age home and your eight-month-old child in the day care for six days a week. Many would do it for seven days a week if they had a choice. Do you have role models who behave differently though? Yes, you do.

Amitabh Bachchan always respected the views of his parents. Having studied in one of the most prestigious schools and university of India, the man remained grounded and respectful. Before he got married to Jaya Bhaduri, he wanted to go to England with her. But his father Dr Harivansh Rai Bachchan advised him to get married before they left. And they did. This is not being backward. Our young men and women might think of this as crass middle-class attitude. They might think disobeying age-old norms is breaking shackles and attaining freedom. But freedom from what? This is the reason why we, as a society, are facing so many socio-psychological problems. We are trying to define modernism in a queer way and yet, we are unable to find peace.

His parents stayed with him till their last days and he did his best to keep them as comfortable as he could. He has fond memories not only of his childhood but also of days when he was struggling as an actor. He posted an emotional eulogy in his blog for his mother, Teji Bachchan, on her birth anniversary.

The actor remembered the support and strength his mother gave him during his 'disastrous days in Bollywood'. He wrote in his blog that his mother sat by him in those disastrous years of his film profession, running her fingers through his hair and reassuring him that all would be well.

He admitted that though she never showed or expressed any emotion in front of the family, she found the absolute moment to express it to him—after the first screening of *Deewaar*. The most touching moment for her was when Amitabh Bachchan dies in the end of the movie. His mother wept for hours like a child for a child she felt had actually passed away in the film. He revealed in his blog that he seeks strength from her and wisdom from his father—in the form of the Ramayan sung in tune, the Hanuman Chalisa rendered by him, and at times the Gurubani that played constantly in the room where his father breathed his last.

He is very much influenced by his father's poetry, philosophy and approach towards life. In most of his interviews, he has recited his poems according to the context and has always quoted his father's teachings which are pearls of wisdom for all of us.

His father is remembered the most for his poem *Madhushala* and Mr Bachchan on numerous occasions is requested to recite it and mostly, he obliges. One line written by his father which he is often heard quoting is, '*Man ka ho toh achcha...na ho toh zyaada achcha! Kyun ki phir wo ishwar ke man ka hota hai, aur ishwar aap ka hamesha achcha chahega!*' (If whatever you desire from your heart happens, it is good, but if it doesn't happen, then it is still better, because then it is the desire of the God and God will always desire something good for you.)

> '*Let parents bequeath to their children not riches, but the spirit of reverence.*'
>
> —Plato

When he was asked about his greatest achievement, Bachchan proudly said the accomplishment he was most proud of was that he was his father's son.

Most of us like to project ourselves as westerners, especially in public eye. But Amitabh Bachchan still refers to his father as 'Babuji' as he fondly remembers his experiences with him in most of his public and media interactions. He demonstrates time and again that he does not suffer from an inferiority complex. I believe that we all must learn this from him. Have faith in yourself, your product and keep your head high in front of the world. Amitabh Bachchan does not like any demonstration of superiority. He does not even like the word 'Bollywood' as to him, it sounds too inferior and reeks of subservience.

He writes about his mother reverently in his blog.

'My Mother, who gave cheer and reason to smile, to all that came in her proximity. My Mother, who fought against caste and creed, tradition and old values, to come and live in an alien land in the heart of conservative Allahabad, with my Father. My Mother, the lioness that would take on an entire gang of thugs who had dared to threaten her children when they were small. My Mother, like all Mothers—the best in the entire universe.'

He religiously follows the practice of visiting the family temple which was built by his father Dr Harivansh Rai Bachchan in the premises of his home, Prateeksha. As a son, he has conserved the sanctity of his parents' room and it is the same as it was when they were alive, revealing his everlasting affection for them.

We believe in the eternal truth that a parent's blessing is the most powerful force. Strength and success is expressed in the term 'Maa ka Ashirwaad' (mother's blessings). Perhaps the reason behind his indestructible determination to come out of his injuries, downfalls and accidents stronger each time was because he loved and cared for his parents who blessed him with all their hearts.

It also brings another aspect of our upbringing into the fore. We say parents who teach good values to their children do them a great favour and are the sole reason why children have values in place. Is that really right?

No, it is not. Parents might give the same 'sanskars' to all their children but it would not be surprising if one becomes a police officer, other a surgeon and yet another, a thug. Therefore, if giving good values is important for parents, it is equally essential for the children to accept them. In this example, two of the children accepted the good values but the third one didn't. They went to the same school, had a similar upbringing and environment but chose to do things differently in life.

If Amitabh Bachchan's parents deserve the credit of bringing up their children well, then equal credit must also be given to him for picking up the good habits from his parents. And the best part is that he is propagating the same ideology and values to the people he interacts with. He is using his fame and name to impart good values to the society and many of us must learn from this.

'Courtesy is as much a mark of a gentleman as courage.'

—Theodore Roosevelt

Courtesy is the King

When you see Amitabh Bachchan during interviews or while delivering a speech, he seems grounded and unassuming. Some people might think that this is acting or false pretence. Even if that is the case, is it really wrong? Your temperament is judged by how you behave, how you speak to others and how you react to questions and participate in a discussion. This is one of the most important parts of Emotional Intelligence—how to display your emotions. Animals can't pretend but we can. If an animal is annoyed, he growls or barks. However, if we are angry, we may choose to smile or at best, not react at all. That is how we are different from animals. We are cultured beings, suave and well-mannered. Courtesy, manners and diplomacy are close cousins. Practised together, they can be the most charming weapon we might possess. If Amitabh Bachchan was going through terrible pain and anxiety during the shooting of KBC, what made him smile and behave politely with the audience? He pulled a chair for a participant every single time and spoke to them with utmost courtesy. It was a sense of responsibility which made him behave this way. He always got up from his chair to welcome all participants and escorted them on the stage.

We sometimes find it hard to be nice even when we are not in pain. Imagine the kind of strength it must have taken for him to behave so kindly during extreme physical and mental discomfort. It is nothing short of incredible. Why can't we all learn to behave like this? His obsession for discipline at all times might be another reason for managing his agony without complaining. In an interview, when he was asked what he hated the most, he said, 'Indiscipline.'

'Bad luck either destroys you...or makes you the man or woman you really are.'

—Amitabh Bachchan

Integrity and Principles: Pillars That Keep You Afloat

During the days when his company ABCL had almost folded up, he kept his chin up and was ready to do his bit to return all his loans. There was an option of filing for bankruptcy but he chose the tough and right path. He didn't want to let down the investors and ensured that all their money was returned. He also never forgot those who helped him in his bad times. He openly acknowledged that Amar Singh stood by him when he was in financial trouble. He is also very fortunate to have a younger brother like him and revealed that he was the one who had introduced him to Anil Ambani. Though they didn't help him financially, they continued to be a great moral support in his time of distress.

Even in the face of his greatest regrets and mistakes, he has demonstrated great courage and conviction. He has learnt to learn from his mistakes. He went through a bad phase and he accepted his failure. But then, he also started afresh. With the chance he got, he decided to prove himself again. In this context, he once said, '*Jo hogaya so hogaya. Hum log chaachch bhi phook phook kar piyenge abhi.*' (Whatever has happened is the past. Today, we are very cautious about everything.)

He was good at creating wealth but was not good at financial matters and thus, he lacked the ability to protect and multiply that wealth. But with tenacity and good values, he fought back and reclaimed his name and money. One can learn a valuable lesson from this—when great people fail, they acknowledge their failures and try to learn from the mistakes they have made in the past. He is a role model for the people who see him as an actor.

He was quite frank when he was asked how the ABCL venture had gone so wrong. He confessed that he was constantly told that he was like a brand figure and was advised to stay out of the nitty-gritty of management. Hence, he had put together an efficient executive team and he entrusted them with the job of running the corporation. He mentioned that his only regret was that despite all the talk about professional executives and professionalism in management, it was a terrible decision as far as the company was concerned. He trusted them but their feedback, their information was inadequate and false. It led to one disaster after another.

This is where we can be inspired and learn from him. If you do not have the requisite competence, especially in fields related to finance and management, you should venture very carefully into business. You cannot remain blind to the commercial part.

The company was launched again by Amitabh Bachchan in 2001 as AB Corp. It proceeded to produce hit films like *Viruddh... Family Comes First* (2005), directed by Mahesh Manjrekar, and *Paa,* directed by R. Balki.

He learnt his lesson—though the hard way.

*'Dusro ki galtiyon se sikhen, aap itne din nahi jee sakte
ki khud itni galtiyan kar sake.' (Learn from the mistakes
of others. You can't live for long enough to make all
mistakes yourself and learn from them.)*

—Amitabh Bachchan

Philanthropy and Giving Back to the Society

*'I think people like Bill Gates, who have given away
enormous sums of money, are shining examples for all of
us to follow.'*

—N.R. Narayana Murthy

It is a known fact that Hollywood celebrities do a lot more for charity than people back home. The same goes for the industrialists abroad. For instance, American singer and songwriter Taylor Swift helped singer Kesha when she needed financial support for a legal battle. Taylor lent her $250,000 during this trying time. The singer also decided to chip in by donating $50,000 to Ascension public schools after heavy floods hit Louisiana.

Angelina Jolie has been involved in issues related to the humanitarian grounds since 2001 and she, along with Brad Pitt, founded the Jolie-Pitt Foundation which has helped establish a centre for children affected with HIV/AIDS and tuberculosis in Ethiopia. They have donated close to five million USD for such causes till now.

One may not be able to recall too many people in the Indian film industry who have helped some of their co-stars when they were in troubled waters or have even participated in social welfare projects. Film industry has no pensions and actors have a short shelf life. If they do not invest wisely or bust up their money when the going is good, they might face problems once they are out of work. However, there have been some good Samaritans of late like Nana Patekar, Akshay Kumar, etc. who have been generous with their money. Amitabh Bachchan has always had a sympathetic attitude towards those who have been beaten down in life and mentions this in several of his interactions with the media.

On an occasion when actor A.K. Hangal who had worked with him in *Sholay* was very unwell, Amitabh Bachchan helped him financially. He did what he could do as a human being. He opened the Harivansh Rai Bachchan Memorial Trust or HRB Memorial Trust in his father's name in 2013. This trust is devoted to human welfare along with spiritual, social, cultural, educational and environmental development.

He explained in an interview that the trust conducts activities with the help of its own initiatives and participates to collect funds for the needy. Over the years, the trust has helped in the rehabilitation of the differently abled, setting up of blood banks, giving medical assistance to patients suffering from cancer and thalassemia, feeding children in schools, sponsoring education, taking care of farmer loans in Andhra and Vidarbha, and so on. He urged people to work independently to better the lives of others.

To help others, he has come forward several times. He donated 30 lakhs ($45,000) to clear the debts of a Vidarbha farmers and 11 lakhs ($16,000) for farmers in Andhra Pradesh. He also donated 25 lakhs ($37,000) to a charitable trust for the upliftment of the girl child in India. Along with this, he was also involved in several projects and missions responsible for social work.

Giving money alone may not be enough, the time you devote to a cause is also important. Signing off a cheque is good but being there and participating in the campaign is much more helpful and noble.

Amitabh was the face of 'Save Our Tigers' campaign initiated by a prominent news channel that promoted the importance of tiger conservation in India. He was also a supporter of PETA and takes pride in the fact they he was a part of a campaign to free an elephant—that was being tortured—from Bannerghatta National Park, near Bangalore.

He was appointed as the UNICEF goodwill ambassador for the polio eradication campaign in India in 2002 as 1,556 polio cases were detected that year. World Health Organization (WHO) declared India a polio-free country in March 2014 with no case of disease reported in the past three years.

I have always told my students that signing off a big cheque and donating it to a charitable foundation is not the only way to do charity. Personal involvement, however small the deed may be, could be more generous. For instance, if you can pick up a puppy shivering in the cold and cover it with a small old rug, it is a wonderful thing to do as a human being. If you can guide someone towards the right stream of education, it is charity for life. You have shaped someone's destiny.

Making a Personal Pitch

At the launch of the tuberculosis awareness campaign in Mumbai, Amitabh Bachchan disclosed that he had contracted tuberculosis in the year 2000. 'I was a TB patient years ago. I have never spoken about it on a public platform, but now is the time. If it could happen to me, it can happen to anyone. I was weak and I had lost appetite. Blood tests revealed that I had TB,' said Bachchan in an interview with *Times of India.*

In his blog, he mentioned how earlier TB patients were sent to sanatoriums but now the best treatment was available for them. He also emphasised on the fact that the treatment should be availed as early as possible. The positive influence of such a statement on the masses is unimaginable.

Mumbai's TB officer, Dr Khetarpal admitted that Bachchan's revelation helped tremendously in getting rid of the stigma attached to the disease. He explained that when a big personality like him accepted he had TB, it had a huge impact on the masses.

'Don't worry when you are not recognized, but strive to be worthy of recognition.'

—Abraham Lincoln

Good Deeds Always Come Back in Full Circle: Recognitions and Honours

When you do so much, achieve so much and deliver so much, you will be rewarded—not only monetarily, but also in terms of fame and name. After a certain amount of money, one doesn't care to count what one has in the bank or how many cars, homes and properties one owns. What becomes important then is if we made any difference. And for some, it is equally essential to know if that difference was acknowledged by the world. I have met so many who are rich and mighty but crave for coverage in the media or are desperate to publish a book! They have it all and yet, they crave for recognition.

After all, no one can deny it—recognition is one of the biggest rewards.

What can you learn from Amitabh about maintaining old values with modern outlook?

1. Respecting one's parents is a sign of culture and good character. Each one of use must learn to look after our parents who did a lot for us throughout our lives. If a person as busy as Amitabh Bachchan can keep his parents close to him, why do some of us think of sending them away to old age homes? Remember, parents' good wishes will always bring you prosperity and happiness.

2. Courtesy doesn't cost us money but earns us a lot of respect. People look up to you if you are nice and polite.

3. Never compromise your integrity. It is everything you have. If you stand by your word, not only will your friends and fraternity help you but even the mighty forces of the universe will come together and support you. Never cheat others; it will never pay in the long run.

4. In case you owe someone something, work hard to earn and return them every penny. Never keep the weight of any obligation on your shoulders.

5. God has given most of us more than what we need. Help those who are not that fortunate. It may not be monitory help, but sometimes moral support is more powerful than materialistic support.

6. Give back to the society, be a good responsible citizen. You will get a lot of satisfaction and respect.

7. Don't look for rewards and awards; do your bit and they will automatically come—one way or the other.

7

SELF-DISCIPLINE

Willpower, Self-control and Delayed Gratification

'One of the most difficult and exasperating words to utter, has perhaps the easiest utterance: NO.'

—Amitabh Bachchan

One of the most essential abilities of a successful person is self-discipline. It is a combination of three qualities—willpower, self-control and delayed gratification.

The ability to work hard and be prepared to wait for the results is the simplest way of defining delayed gratification. Self-control, which is the ability to say 'no' to a temptation, is God's gift to some extent but to a large extent, it can be consciously developed. This is highly important because the mental strength of an individual depends on the spirit of that individual. Let us consider the students who prepare for the civil services examination or IIT entrance tests. Those who are determined to work hard can forgo simple temptations like an interesting TV show, a party or a family function. As an evidence of unbeatable determination, some of those who fail in the first attempt try again the next year with the same or more vigour.

Today, we live in the times of instant gratification. We want a file to be uploaded in a few seconds, a computer to boot instantly, a WhatsApp message to be acknowledged right away, burger or pizza to arrive in 30 minutes and we prefer instant noodles over a properly cooked meal. We have lost our ability to be patient and wait for our turn calmly.

Do you know why weight loss programmes fail? In most cases, it happens because one cannot say no to good food, a pizza or a burger. The second reason is the inability to work hard every day on a low calorie diet and wait for two months for the results to show. The first one is related to willpower and self-control while the second one is delayed gratification. Life is not an instant geyser where you push a button and hot water starts pouring out. You need to put in consistent efforts for a period of time before you can even think of achieving something.

Many religions recommend fasting in some form or the other. The idea is to build a strong character, will to control oneself and install a sense of self-discipline in the person. Cleansing of the body and digestive system is just a collateral benefit.

'Willpower is the art of replacing one habit for another.'

—Michael Garofalo

Willpower and Patience Demonstrated by Amitabh Bachchan

Many actors work on their physique and have to quickly lose or gain weight for a role. But there are few who take it as a simple challenge without any commercial, professional or even medical compulsion to do so.

Big B has done such things for reasons most cannot comprehend. To have sensible food habits is something which always works in the favour of our health. But quitting bad habits and adopting a healthier lifestyle is not easy. It requires a strong willpower and determination to say 'no' to good food, especially the food you love. Amitabh Bachchan, like all of us, loved food and had a sweet tooth. He was very fond of jalebi and kheer. He liked alcohol and smoking as well. But on one social event, someone taunted, 'You will never be able to leave smoking and drinking.' Amitabh immediately decided to quit both and he did. It has been more than 40 years since that incident. He also turned vegetarian, not because of any medical or religious reason, but because he felt it would be better to be a vegetarian and change his eating habits. The man does not eat chocolates, does not drink coffee or tea and does not even have aerated drinks. This is leading a Spartan life and in an industry which believes in partying hard all the time, it must require a strong willpower.

The Vice President of Human Resources at Reliance Jio, Harjeet Khanduja recalled his brief interaction with Mr Bachchan where he noticed some revealing traits of the superstar. The first thing he noticed was that Mr Bachchan has tremendous amount of patience. He saw people hugging him, clicking selfies, some even touching his feet and he was ready to interact with every one without displaying any signs of haste.

He was very impressed with his temperament and described how everyone wanted to prove that they were his biggest fans. People recited his dialogues and the poems of his father. He was requested to recite them too. He often corrected people when they recited the incorrect words of the poem with immense humility and politeness. After the interaction, Khanduja was to receive a signed copy of *Madhushala*. Bachchan had signed around 80 copies beforehand. But somehow it took time to bring one more copy. He was animated due to the delay. Khanduja could see the urge for perfection in his actions.

Being Organized is a Part of Self-discipline

As a teacher of management studies, I always say that management is nothing more than common sense. Mr Bachchan is not only punctual but is also pretty conscious of optimizing his activities. He uses common sense to do such things. For instance, in an interview, he revealed that he had to use reading glasses without which he could not manage. To ensure that he didn't keep looking for them, he said he kept several pairs at home in different places—on the bedside table, in the sitting area, next to the sofa in the drawing room or on a table in the balcony. I do the same. I keep a pair in my briefcase, on my office table, in my car and at least in three different rooms at home, including one in the toilet. It doesn't cost much and is very convenient.

Amitabh Bachchan also mentioned that they have subscribed to several newspapers at home where he lives with his wife Jaya Bachchan, son Abhishek Bachchan and daughter-in-law Aishwarya Rai Bachchan. To ensure that the papers are circulated to all of them, they have a post-it stuck to each newspaper which carries names of the members of the family and as and when each of them reads it, they put a tick in front of their names. This is brilliant.

I have worked with people who are very prompt and meticulous. One look at their office desk can help you make out if they are neat and clean in their outlook. With an organized person, everything will be where it should be. Even in their briefcases, pens, pencils, blank sheets and all the stuff required for a working professional are placed appropriately. On the other hand, have you seen disorganized toilets? They are the most annoying for any sane person. How can you leave your personal things like toothbrush, shaving cream, shampoos and perfumes scattered on the sink with the towels jumbled up? This is nothing short of being uncouth. I have always believed that an organization can be judged by the cleanliness and maintenance of their toilets.

A Lesson or Two from the Military Ethos

Amitabh Bachchan played the role of an army officer in the movie *Major Saab* (1998), most of which was shot on the sprawling 8000 acres campus of National Defence Academy, Khadakvasla. He got to learn how well-disciplined the armed forces were and the way routine was instilled in the officers of the three services at this phenomenal institute.

After a few years, while addressing the cadets at the academy where he was the guest speaker, he was all praises for discipline and its importance in our lives. While delivering his speech, he was very candid about how much he respected the armed forces. He praised the institution and declared that if there was any way in which the most required ingredient of discipline could be executed within us, it was through the portals of institutions such as the NDA.

Khushwant and Amitabh: Diverse Yet Alike

On the face of it, Mr Khushwant Singh, the late writer and journalist looked pretty 'bindas', but in reality, he was as fastidious as Mr Bachchan as far as diet, timing and regimen were concerned. People who dined at his place say that the liquor would be served up to a given time and as soon as the time was up, dinner was served. And the host Khushwant Singh would himself announce the end of the party by saying, 'The party is over. Good night folks.'

He would get up at 4 a.m. to write his columns or his books and was very disciplined when it came to diet and deadlines. These are the things creative people must learn from other creative people. There is a misconception amongst those who 'feel' they are creative. They think if you are creative, you need to look disorderly, wear weird clothes or have a funky look. It somehow excuses you to be irresponsible in your professional space and above all, throw tantrums. This is far from true.

Such pseudo ideas about creativity are what we need to change.

> *'Let's ask God to help us to self-control for one who lacks it, lacks his grace.'*

—Rumi

Turning Failure into Success

Amitabh Bachchan overcame two phases of life: when he struggled and gained his fame, fortune and popularity; and when he had everything, only to lose it all. He survived the struggle and regained all that he had lost. Discipline, self-control and willpower played a great role in his rise from the ashes like a phoenix, and that too, twice over.

Many of us, like Amitabh Bachchan, fail at some point of time in our lives. Is it, then, possible to take yourselves out of the muddy slushy quicksand of a failure pit?

Here are a few tips.

1. **Count your strengths**

   At the time when you are emotionally down, there is a need to pull yourself up. You need to console yourself. Life is a rollercoaster ride; it has its ups and downs. Handling yourself on this ride is the essence of your strength and resilience. You need to find your own healing balm and there is nothing better than looking back at your previous achievements. Don't depend on your past laurels to rescue you but use them to help you get in the right frame of mind by focusing on the strengths that made you achieve all that in the first place.

2. **Time is the greatest healing factor**

   Don't write yourself off right away. Lick your emotional wounds and give yourself some time. It may take a week, sometimes even months to reconcile and recover. Do not take any action in haste. Think about what you are best at and the options available to you for an action plan. Take failure as a mentor, not a demon or an enemy.

3. **You have not failed**

   Failure should be not taken as irreversible. Look at it as a project and don't be too hard on yourself.

4. **Talk to yourself**

   When bad things happen, one tends to get into a shell. But it is natural. If you say positive things to yourself, your mood will improve. Instead of saying, 'I have failed miserably', you say, 'This time I didn't succeed, but I can do better later on.' This will help you mount the horse once again and ride along.

5. **Take a five-year test**

   This works beautifully. Think of the failure moving forward five years in life and then look back and imagine its significance. You will realize that after five years, most of the failures or losses of today will seem insignificant. And then you will understand how the problem has been blown out of proportion by you in your mind. We often tend to make failure look larger than life and bigger than what they actually are.

'Don't worry about genius and don't worry about not being clever. Trust rather to hard work, perseverance, and determination. The best motto for a long march is "Don't grumble. Plug on."'

—Sir Frederick Treves

What can you learn from Amitabh on self-discipline?

1. Learn to say 'no' to your desires. If someone offers you stuff which looks good but you feel it is not good for you, have the strength to refuse it.
2. Develop patience as a habit. It is possible. If a person like Mr Bachchan with so many health issues can be patient with his fans and co-stars, why can we not achieve that?
3. Get yourself organized to be more effective and comfortable. Organized people seldom find themselves in a helpless situation.
4. Make your rules, follow them and let others also follow them according to your schedule. You will be respected for this.
5. Admire those who admire discipline. This will make you stronger in your convictions as far as self-discipline is concerned.

8

PROFESSIONALISM AND WORK ETHICS

Competence, Teamwork and Constructive Criticism

'Once you realize that you're in something that you've always wanted and you don't want to lose it, you behave differently. And that means the integrity, the professionalism, and knowing what's right from wrong and still making choices that you probably wouldn't have made.'

—Paul Anka

Why Is Professionalism Important?

Being true to your work is a cardinal principle without which you can never be successful. Either you take a job that you love or start loving the job you take. Sportsmen, men in uniform, marketing professionals, consultants, doctors, singers, teachers, mountaineers—it is true for every profession under the sun.

Once you like your job and you are sincere in what you do, there is very little that can stop you from progressing in your career. Being professionally dedicated earns you respect not only from your bosses but also from peers, subordinates and clients. People want to work willingly with those who tend to be good at their work and also take their work seriously.

When you're in a profession, it is important to understand that it is your bread and butter—your 'rozi roti'—and you cannot be dishonest with that. When you are paid for something, you must give your paymaster the services he has paid for. You must deliver to his satisfaction. As they say, 'Work is worship'.

Let Us Understand the Meaning of Professionalism As Understood by the Corporate World First

Cinema is now known as film industry which broadly falls under the overall ambit of corporate ethics and professional acumen. So what applies to an industry in general applies to the film industry as well. Professionalism is often defined as the strict adherence to courtesy, honesty and responsibility when dealing with individuals or other companies in a business environment. This trait often includes high level of excellence above and beyond basic requirements. Work ethics are usually concerned with the personal values demonstrated by business owners, corporate or entrepreneurs which are further instilled in the company's employees. Good work ethics may include completing tasks in a timely manner with the highest quality possible and taking pride in completed tasks. Professionalism encompasses a number of different attributes and together, these attributes identify and define a professional.

Specialized Domain Knowledge

- Keep yourself updated: Master your craft so that others want to work with you and even under you.
- Competency: Be reliable and dependable. It relates to your expertise and ability to deliver.
- Honesty, integrity and accountability: Keep your word, demonstrate integrity, be humble and accept your mistakes. You are accountable for your deliverables. If you falter, you must take the responsibility.
- Self-regulation: It is important to accept and correct mistakes. You should be a self-starter and manage your obligations without people telling you.

Professional actors who take these attributes in the right spirit go a long way. Amitabh Bachchan is one of them. Directors, choreographers, lyricists, producers, scriptwriters, dialogue writers and co-stars—everybody feels this about him. The basic tenet is that a film is about a director's vision and an actor is supposed to fulfil that dream by delivering what the director has in mind. A director, too, takes out the best in a capable actor.

An actor as versatile as Amitabh Bachchan is like a kaleidoscope. One can see different colours and hues in the different roles he plays. It is up to the director to extract what he wants out of him. It is like a cup full of pure honey from which a bee can take however much it wants. It completely depends on the bee. For instance, Hrishikesh Mukherjee got serious performances as well as delightful comedy out of him. He knew that the actor had an unimaginable range.

Amitabh Bachchan was a nine-film flop hero when Prakash Mehra launched him in *Zanjeer*. He knew the potential and that is why he took the risk. Salim-Javed crafted the script and Prakash Mehra translated it on the screen while Bachchan gave a 10 on 10 performance to create the blockbuster.

Prakash Mehra understood his strengths and used them in all his subsequent movies. *Muqaddar Ka Sikandar* (1978) and *Namak Halaal* (1982) along with other movies featured him in emotional roles which were controlled and measured, yet hard-hitting.

He understood the actor's ability to emote controlled coiled anger in *Zanjeer*, suppressed seething hate in *Trishul* (1978) or unexpressed love in *Shakti* (1982). It was never over the top; always precise. All these performances have been etched in the audience's memory forever.

Amitabh in one interview admitted that Manmohan Desai and Prakash Mehra were two directors who could take the best out of him. Both understood that his intensity was his strength as an actor. His performance as a drunkard is unmatched even today. Manmohan Desai's *Amar Akbar Anthony* where he talks to the mirror is something that will remain eternal in Hindi cinema. *Satte Pe Satta* directed by Raj N. Sippy and *Do Anjane* (1976), directed by Dulal Guha also channelized his talent very well. He appears in a dozen films enacting a 'sharabi', sozzled and drunk, each performance better than the other.

Though not a dancer in the traditional sense, he had a sense of rhythm which could be used along with his lanky frame to cull out a dance number effectively and this was done by several directors. Ram Gopal Varma did greats films like

Sarkar with him and he is full of praises for Amitabh Bachchan. He stressed on the fact that Amitabh Bachchan was an actor who could create an impactful scene literally out of smoke. He offered him tailor-made roles that went with his age.

Amongst the latest directors, Shoojit Sircar who worked with Mr Bachchan on two back-to-back projects *Piku* and *Pink* is full of admiration for him. He thinks he is an intelligent person who understands the script and role quickly and if he is convinced, he says yes immediately. When *Piku* was almost ready, they were looking for someone for the role of a lawyer in his next venture *Pink*. They decided to approach Mr Bachchan and narrated the script to him. Within five minutes of the narration, he said, 'Let's shoot.'

R. Balki has also worked with him in several films and considers him the country's greatest actor. Balki directed Bachchan in *Cheeni Kum, Paa* and *Shamitabh*—all are critically acclaimed and offer Amitabh Bachchan in completely diverse roles.

'Indian actor Amitabh Bachchan has the combined star wattage of Brando, De Niro and Eastwood, and is loved by millions.'

—Independent (9 February 2015)

Writer's Delight

Directors and writers love him so much that some even write roles specifically for him. They might do it inadvertently or may not admit it but they always have it in the back of their minds. They have made *Black*, *Khakee*, *Kabhi Alvida Naa Kehna*, *Kabhi Khushi Kabhie Gham...*, *Pink* and *Piku* with him as the center figure—tall and towering.

Javed Akhtar, the lyricist and story writer said that talented people like Amitabh Bachchan were very rare. The kind of work he had done and the example he had set through his work in all these years was an inspiration to all. He mentioned how he thought he was very fortunate to have worked with him for many years in 13 to 14 films. He added that they had started their career together, and today he had carved a niche for himself and was doing amazingly well.

'This could be something controversial I say but leave aside actors like Dilip Kumar, Bajraj Sahni or Amitabh Bachchan, who were brilliant actors, I don't think that currently there is any actor who is of the standard of these actors,' he said at a media interaction during a seminar on 'Perfecting Indian Cinema'.

> *'I like to feel the butterflies in the stomach; I like to go home and have a restless night and wonder how I'm going to be able to accomplish this feat, get jittery. That hunger and those butterflies in the stomach are very essential for all creative people.'*
>
> —Amitabh Bachchan

Learning Is a Passion

This is one area we need to work on as a nation. For more than two decades as part of my work, I have been dealing closely with young budding managers as well as senior executives including CEOs and MDs who run large companies. More often than not, across the board, I was disappointed that work was not taken seriously—not seriously enough. In the same breath, I would like to specifically talk about the young professionals who are just getting into the business arena. They look at a job as a way to earn money, benefits and comfort. Very little effort is put towards learning and delivering what one has been hired for. In a global economy, can we afford to compete with the rest of the world with this attitude? I am afraid not.

In the entertainment industry, especially cinema, the scenario is different. Those who want to outshine others and survive the tough competition career in showbiz often give their 100 per cent, sometimes even more than that. New actors, singers and directors struggle to make a mark for themselves. One can observe a significant rise in talent, hard work and adventurous attitude in the younger lot. A lot can be attributed to the increase in opportunities and platforms. It is also a question of survival of the fittest. Therefore, in the creative field, people work hard to get ahead. But only hard work is not enough to sustain success over a period of time. This is where professionalism steps in. Firstly, success is very heady and one must be grounded at all times. Secondly, you cannot let your guards down even for a moment. You need to work hard every day to stay in the position you have reached. It is like running on a treadmill. You have to maintain your speed. Can the youngsters or entrepreneurs entering the corporate arena learn a lesson or two from AB? Yes, a lot can be learnt from the stalwart, especially on professionalism.

*'I'm just an actor, and if I can leave something behind
that my kids will be proud of, then that's what
I want. I don't want my kids to be
embarrassed by anything I've done.'*

—Johnny Depp

Competence and Creativity: That 5 Per Cent Grey Area

*'The difference between the almost right word and the
right word is really a large matter—'tis the difference
between the lightning bug and the lightning.'*

—Mark Twain

Amitabh Bachchan is a performer who has learnt the tricks of the trade on field. He never received any formal training in acting. This is commendable. He learnt and improved his craft bit by bit—always outperforming himself and doing better than his earlier appearances. In one of his interviews, he admitted that he doesn't quite know what happens to him when he comes in front of the camera. For him, everything falls in place only then and he is able to deliver his dialogues effortlessly.

If one analyses the acumen of the greatest singers and the great ones, the difference is very little. All successful singers have a good voice, range, idea of rhythm, scale and sense of 'sur' and 'taal'. Yet there is no one like Kishore Kumar or Mohammed Rafi. That slight difference which I would like to call 'the last 5 per cent' is difficult to explain in words and is also tough if not impossible to achieve. That additional pinch of exclusivity is the most important and that is what makes a superstar stand out amongst all the other stars.

In an interview, Javed Akhtar said that Kishore Kumar had a certain type of 'sophistication' in his voice. How brilliantly put! It is true. You can witness this when you listen to his songs. It is the same with actors. It all boils down to that 5 per cent difference which can be perceived but cannot be defined and remains a grey area in the realm of creativity. It is true for storytellers too. Why are Jeffry Archer, Daniel Defoe, J.K. Rowling, Mark Twain and H.G. Wells topping the charts amongst millions of writer? It is because they have that 5 per cent of charismatic difference. Amitabh Bachchan's overall performance is that kind of an end product which stuns you with its undefinable difference.

Teamwork and Dedication

Amitabh Bachchan is prepared to give as many retakes as required to get the right shot. He is always prepared to go that extra mile. In 2001, while shooting for *Aks,* despite his muscle disorder, he performed a dangerous stunt. He jumped from a height of 30 feet. He tried to give his best even when he was drained and exhausted. Similarly, for *Shootout at Lokhandwala,* he recorded 23 scenes in five hours. Which director and co-star will not be delighted with this kind of dedication?

He is a team player and understands how new artists can feel intimidated by his very presence. Everyone looks up to him and when they see him approaching, many are left awestruck and in shock. But Amitabh Bachchan does his best to make his co-actors feel comfortable. While shooting for *Pink*, he mingled with the newcomers even off the sets, just to make sure they achieved a level of comfort with him.

Product Positioning and Product Lifecycle

> *'By nature, I keep moving, man. My theory is, be the shark. You've just got to keep moving. You can't stop.'*

—Brad Pitt

If an actor is seen as a product, Amitabh Bachchan was actually re-launched with Prakash Mehra's *Zanjeer* in 1973. He has lasted almost four generations of actors. He started with Vinod Khanna, Rajesh Khanna, Shashi Kapoor and Dharmendra as his contemporaries and as he moved forward, he appeared opposite Randhir Kapoor, Rishi Kapoor, Govinda and Mithun Chakraborty. The next decade saw the rise of Akshay Kumar, Anil Kapoor and Sunny Deol. And before we knew it, he was also working with the Khans. If this wasn't enough, he has also starred with the recent actors the likes of Ranveer Singh, Ranbir Kapoor and Riteish Deshmukh.

A product goes through four phases: introduction (launch), growth, maturity and decline. Amitabh was at his peak i.e. maturity in the mid-80s and soon after, his decline began. A typical product would have phased out at this point and a new product would have been launched. Modification or tweaking doesn't usually work. Mr Bachchan first tried to revive himself with the help of his name and popularity but as he was aging, it didn't work for him. This was the time he acted in films like *Major Saab* and could not do much about his declining popularity.

There was only one way. He had to relaunch himself as a new product. He did that with TV as a medium and KBC became his comeback. Indian TV had never seen such a big star and that was the game changer for him and the production house. Of course, his acting talent remained intact and the show was a hit. This is how Amitabh Bachchan relaunched himself as a new product—in a new avatar. From big screen to small, it was a great transition.

He came up with his trademark French white beard and black hair which not only worked for him but suited his age too.

Along with KBC, he started appearing in every possible advertisement—from hair oil, chocolates, cement, Boroplus creams to different brands of cars. This gave him access to every household. The interest of the audience was rapidly growing and so was the market.

He used the blitzkrieg strategy for a relaunch on the big screen. It was rapid fire mode. Soon, he was doing more films than he had in the '80s and roles were being written specifically for him. Appearing in advertisements made sure he was everywhere. It was a face no one could forget. Apart from a host of commercial products, he also became the brand ambassador for Gujarat, polio vaccination, fight against TB, Save the Tiger campaign, Beti Bachao, Beti Padhao, and Swachch Bharat. Whether it was commercial ads or social messages, he did it all!

Everything has worked for him since that relaunch. TV,

commercials, new roles and social initiatives generated synergy in the critical mass, turning the tables in his favour. It also gave him the lift he urgently required.

Honesty, Integrity and Accountability

Being open to criticism:

This is what every individual regardless of the type of profession he is in must stand by. Success in creative field can get very dangerous. It sometimes delivers a knockout punch, especially if one is not ready for it. Actors turned stars can literally see stars in the day because of the kind of public adulation one experiences in a very short period. They are catapulted to a position they feel is godly.

They begin refusing inputs and feedback to improve or correct themselves. That is the doom's day for a creative person. Your family can be the biggest leveller, provided you listen to them and they are honest enough to tell you of your follies.

Amitabh Bachchan in an interview said that after a release, the entire family goes to his daughter Shweta to get her real reaction to the movie. She always gives them feedback on their songs and movies. And 99.9 per cent of the time, she is bang on. All of them have a private thing amongst themselves that if Shweta endorses a film or a song, they're in safe hands. As for his wife, Jaya Bachchan, he feels that because she was trained at FTII, she looks at the craft in a holistic way—in terms of editing, script, sound and screenplay. He also feels that she is cautious with her compliments. She won't say anything unless she really likes something. As far as he is concerned, he judges his own performance and looks for any scope for improvement. He assesses the overall quality of the film.

'All that attention to the perfect lighting, the perfect this, the perfect that, I find terribly annoying.'

—Meryl Streep

Self-regulation

Leveraging your strengths and weaknesses:

Every actor must identify his/her strengths and weaknesses. The winner is the one who not only leverages his strengths but also uses his weak points to his advantage. Amitabh Bachchan too has his weaknesses. He has a lanky frame and very long arms which can look disproportional and odd when taken from some specific camera angles. He found a clever way of putting his hands in his pockets when he had to walk in some of the scenes and made it his style statement. He also developed his signature pose—with one hand on the waist and the other arm waving in the front while delivering an intense dialogue. He made full use of his long legs by exploiting the bell-bottoms of the '70s and mid-80s. He allowed the directors to use his legs while shooting some scenes of the actor running, making him look larger than life, especially in slow motion.

Nobody can dispute the quality of his voice. Morgan Freeman, Peter O'Toole or ever Richard Harris may have had the most mesmerizing voice in Hollywood but Amitabh Bachchan's voice has a texture no one can match.

He is an actor who doesn't have the conventional good looks of a film star, has a thin lanky frame, long arms and is too tall for Indian standards. But he used all these features to his advantage and became one of the greatest performers entirely on his acting prowess.

Professional to the Core

People who are not in the field of cinema may not realize how much an actor works for every film that he undertakes. He is prepared to give retakes as and when required by the director, has to act and dance in all types of weather conditions and wear make-up and costumes required for the character. It doesn't matter if it is raining or snowing, if it is hot or humid, the work must go on. While the movie is being made, actors have no idea about its future or fate in the box office, yet, they give their best.

Amitabh Bachchan also gives his best to satisfy the director and justify the script. He is always ready with full costume and make-up on, without needing anyone to remind him. His attitude saves production cost, allows peace in sets and between the co-stars. After all this, who would not like to have him on board?

'I don't use any techniques; I'm not trained to be an actor. I just enjoy working in films.'

—Amitabh Bachchan

9

CHARISMA AND PANACHE
Personality, Humility and Sophistication

'One should either be a work of art,
or wear a work of art.'

—Oscar Wilde

Charisma is something which cannot be easily defined or explained. One can always recall having met people who had a magnetic personality. Their very presence inspires confidence and motivates people to follow them out of respect. Such people—men and women—have charismatic personalities.

What happens when you see someone like this? When they enter a room, people get up in respect, when they cross your path, heads turn. When you are with them, it is reassuring. In human virtuosity, this factor is easily achievable. People often debate whether it is an inborn thing or if it can be acquired. I feel it is a mix of both.

You may or may not have a little of it in yourself but over a period of time, you can develop it. It need not come with authority alone and it may not even come with achievement. It is grace that comes naturally to some and dawns upon others with experience. It also has a lot to do with the way you carry yourself, articulate, speak and how sophisticated you can be.

Panache, flamboyance and verve go hand in hand. But it is not rumbustious, rowdy or boisterous. It is never in your face. In contrast, it is subtle, smooth and graceful. It can neither be heard nor seen, it can only be felt. It is like magnetic induction.

Greats like Barak Obama, John F. Kennedy, Mahatma Gandhi, Winston Churchill and Indira Gandhi had this. Narendra Modi has it too. Martin Luther King, Swami Vivekananda and Osho also had something which people were attracted to. In the acting fraternity, people who possess this attribute are Clint Eastwood, Jack Nicholson, Al Pacino, Sean Connery, Marlon Brando, Richard Burton, Morgan Freeman, Robert De Niro and Yul Bryner—they have great charm and stage presence. Amongst actresses, the list is endless—Meryl Streep, Julia Roberts, Kate Winslet and of course, Elizabeth Taylor, Sophia Loren and Marilyn Monroe. In the Indian context, it would be Madhubala, Suchitra Sen, Nutan and Vyjayanthimala.

When we talk about army top brass, many names come to mind—Field Marshal S.H.F.J. Manekshaw, General William Slim, General Douglas MacArthur, General George S. Patton, George Washington and General Bernard Montgomery.

In French, charisma is known as 'Je ne Sais quoi' meaning

'I know not what'. It has several components—oratory, dramatization, ability to adapt, emotional connection, grace and style. In what proportion which ingredient is required, it is difficult to tell. That varies from person to person—what works for you may not work for me. At the end of the day, how you carry yourself, what you speak and how you speak it is what matters.

Amitabh Bachchan initially thought he was not a conventionally good-looking man with a lanky frame and one drooping shoulder. Did he acquire charisma after his first hit? Or after five hits? No, it was much later. It was a culmination of his maturity, fighting spirit, command over languages, way of carrying himself and pulling off whatever he wore. It was his measured response in front of media, punctuality, professionalism, diplomacy, humility, honesty and acting. All this and much more.

Sophistication

Whether he wears a suit or a kurta pyjama, he always looks nice and sophisticated. He may wear a track suit in *Pink*, a coolie's uniform in *Deewaar* or bell-bottomed trousers, he still looks impactful. His anger is never overboard, ugly or dirty. Other actors mix anger with arrogance when performing onscreen. Amitabh's anger is always mixed with hurt and tears. His annoyance also has that touch of class. He can easily position himself equal to his opponent, even when he is shown on a higher and a more powerful platform.

Javed Akhtar described it beautifully when he said that

the most thrilling aspect of his confrontational scenes was not just his physical courage but his easy assumption of equality. He mentioned how Bachchan as an actor never felt outclassed. While playing proletarian characters too, he always walked with the panache of an aristocrat. He added that there was a certain grace about the characters he had played. Many actors had tried to ape Amitabh but they had all failed because they didn't have the sophistication and the 'tehzeeb' (culture and good manners) that he grew up with.

> *'With any part you play, there is a certain amount of yourself in it. There has to be, otherwise it's just not acting. It's lying.'*

—Johnny Depp

Down to Earth

When his business venture ABCL collapsed, he was really down and under. He once mentioned in an interview that there was a day when he reached his office at 4 a.m. and began thinking of a way out of the mess. He asked himself what he was good at. Acting was the immediate reply. It was the only thing he knew. He needed work. He wanted a role to play in a film. That is when he approached Mr Yash Chopra who lived behind his house. At 4 a.m. in the morning, he told him that he needed work.

Mr Chpora called him straightaway and gave him a powerful role in his next movie *Mohabbatein*. It gave

Amitabh the much-needed break that could put him back into mainstream cinema. He was a megastar and accepting a role of an old man must not have been easy for a guy like him. But he understood the need of the hour and walked up to Chopra, knowing fully well that earlier people used to queue in to meet Amitabh. He had to adapt, the situation called for it. And this adaptability is what eventually brought success for him.

In an interview, he was asked if he was considering a biopic on himself. He responded by saying that he didn't have enough to merit a biopic. But he added that a good series could be made on the works of his father based on his literary contribution and poetry.

Panache

Even when he plays an underdog, there is always a streak of being equal. In the movie *Deewaar*, in a coolie's uniform with a badge, bidi between the lips, he looks into the eyes of the villains sitting in their plush cars and manages to look suave and well-mannered. He says, '*Main aaj bhi phenke hue paise nahi uthata*,' (Even today, I don't pick up money thrown on the ground at me) when the man throws a wad of notes on the table for him. As a goon also, he looked like a sophisticated gangster. It is not what you wear; it is how you carry it that matters.

In *Bunty Aur Babli* (2005), he played the role of a cop wearing dark glasses with leather jacket and his character kept on twisting and turning his neck which was not easy to pull off. He, despite not being a great dancer in the classical sense, managed to make a mark with his incredible performance.

His look with a hat in *The Great Gatsby* was a real stunner. *MensXp* magazine, in 2015, featured him as the most stylish man who could carry a chic jacket to a pinstriped suit with equal grace and élan. In the song 'Birju' of Ajay Chandhok's *Hey Bro* (2015), he was seen dancing with Prabhu Deva, Ajay Devgn, Hrithik Roshan and Ganesh Acharya—all accomplished dancers and choreographers—and his stylish performance proved that Amitabh was the one who added the 'special' to the special appearances. In *Deewaar*, he handled the sudden transformation from a porter to a sophisticated don wearing a polka dot bow and a dinner jacket so convincingly.

No wonder women still love him, even at 75. A recent study was conducted to find out the most important criterion sought out by single men and women when searching for their life partner. The participants also had to choose a celebrity who matched their desired quality. In the survey, 62.7 per cent women voted for Amitabh Bachchan as their ideal partner.

'*Yeh panache nahi to kya hai?*' (If this is not panache, then what is?)

People are In Awe of Him

Karan Johar, in an interview revealed that he grew up in Malabar Hill in Bombay and his father was a film producer. So, he was used to seeing stars coming over. But Amitabh Bachchan's magnetism was something else. He couldn't help but stand up when he entered a room. Since the age of four, whenever he saw him, he would get up and touch his feet. Karan Johar joked about how Shweta and Abhishek keep teasing him but he couldn't help it. It was like he was on autopilot mode. He could be anywhere in the world but he had to do it whenever he saw him. That's the kind of reverence and respect he has for him.

Talking about his charismatic persona, he added that Amitabh Bachchan's towering personality, height, baritone, good command over two languages (Hindi and English), humongous sense of culture and tradition, sense of dignity— all this had made him the icon he is today. He has that stature, both literally and otherwise. Even if he walked into a room in Czechoslovakia, everyone in that room would know he was someone famous. Whenever he walks into a room, one automatically feels one should get up and clap. His incredible consistency is admirable. Even when he was down, he never crumbled. He was silent. He never showed any sense of insecurity. He never made himself vulnerable. And he always rose like a Phoenix. He handled those periods with such grace. After his comeback with *Kaun Banega Crorepati*, he emerged as the patriarch of the nation. No one can host a show like he can. His fluency in Hindi is incredible. In a land where the national language is abused, he makes it sound exotic.

The admiration Karan Johar harbours for Big B was evident when he narrated an incident that took place while he was directing him in *Kabhi Khushi Kabhie Gham...* The idea of directing Big B was so overwhelming that he had fainted on the first day of shoot. He had a doctor on the set at all times because he had wound himself up so much. When he recovered consciousness, Bachchan was sitting in front of him. He said to him, 'Don't worry, I'll dance well!' In terms of direction, Johar said that one had to simply explain a scene to him and that would be all. He was beyond any instruction.

Karan Johar further talked about his position amongst the actors and said that Mr Bachchan's stardom was blessed by the universe. There was divinity about it.

It is true that in the film industry, maintenance and survival are the only two things that matter. Today, he's an even bigger movie star than he ever was. A 10-year-old knows him. A 70-year-old knows him. He has stood the test of time.

Javed Akhtar, who has worked with him in more than a dozen films, talked about his adaptability as well as humility. He described his performance in *Shakti* where he played the son to Dilip Kumar. Akhtar recounted in an interview that despite being a megastar, he did not let his stardom come in the way of playing the role of the son. He looked submissive, passive, frightened and intimidated—just how a son should look in front of a powerful father. He demonstrated that he is an actor first and then a star. He added that Bachchan deliberately damped down his trademark fiery acting style in order to harmonize with Dilip Kumar's understated naturalism. That is the mark of a true star.

There have, however, been some weak performances. After all, no one is perfect. Amitabh Bachchan looked like a wax dummy in some of his post-comeback films. But in them too, he has played pivotal characters. As the rigid headmaster of an exclusive men's college in *Mohabbatein*, he looks more like someone carved in granite. He worked hard to serve the director's conception of his character—a man so stiffened by disappointment that he looked virtually immobile. It actually worked for the movie as he looked like a strange visitor from another era.

In *Pink*, he delivered powerful courtroom drama scenes which probably no one else could have pulled off with such élan. He discussed sensitive issues without making it seem vulgar. On the other side of the spectrum, he also played the role of a constipated old man in *Piku* and even with great actors like Irrfan Khan sharing the screen, he managed to take the cake. Just imagine, a movie revolving around constipation. You need to have courage and confidence to accept such roles and deliver a stellar performance. It cannot be denied that even in his sunset years, he looks mightier and brighter than ever.

Looking at his difficult journey, he said, 'The amount of things I have been through and the remarkable ways in which the body has reacted is just phenomenal. No wonder I became religious, because you don't know why something's happening to you and you don't know how you bounced back.'

'Courage is grace under pressure.'

—Ernest Hemingway

Being Grateful

A great man is someone who does not forget his roots and makes sure that the success does not go to his head. Amitabh Bachchan enjoys his success but has his feet firmly on the ground. He once said that Sunday evenings when people gather around his house to show their support and affection act like adrenaline for him. It is a constant source of motivation for him. He is surprised at how this has lasted for so long. 1982 to 2010—that is 28 years! He believes that God has been kind and very gracious.

'Fashion changes, but style endures.'

—Coco Chanel

What can you learn from Amitabh on having a good personality and charisma?

1. Some people have a bit of charisma given to them by God, while others build it with effort and a bit of luck.
2. Charisma comes when you earn respect in your professional and personal life and when people hold you in high esteem.
3. Sophistication is a part of charisma and panache. One needs to have good education, upbringing and a conscious effort to move in this direction.
4. Whatever you do, do it in style.
5. Religious gurus who had a clearly defined philosophy with a sense of commitment earned huge respect. Those who didn't perished very soon.
6. A well-mannered cultured person always earns respect and people think twice before saying something derogatory about him.
7. Being cultured, diplomatic and respectful is the starting point towards acquiring respect. Remember, you don't demand respect, you command it.

BIBLIOGRAPHY

1. http://www.glamsham.com/movies/news/14/mar/07-news-amitabh-bachchan-infused-virtues-of-humility-in-anupam-kher-031402.asp
2. http://indiatoday.intoday.in/story/amitabh-bachchan-interview-big-b-bollywood/1/242033.html\
3. https://www.bemoneyaware.com/blog/amitabh-bachchan-from-bankruptcy-to-crorepati/
4. https://libquotes.com/amitabh-bachchan/quote/lbp3n7b
5. http://www.bollywoodpresents.com/rare-interview-of-amitabh-bachchan-and-rajesh-khanna-episode-2.html
6. http://www.bollywoodlife.com/news-gossip/amitabh-bachchan-professionally-i-am-fond-of-deepika-padukone/
7. http://www.biscoot.com/news/bollywood-news-deepika-on-cloud-nine-16838/ds
8. http://www.catchnews.com/regional-cinema/rajinikanth-is-the-real-boss-of-indian-cinema-says-amitabh-bachchan-rajinikanth-latest-news-1469758319.html
9. http://www.filmfare.com/interviews/dilip-kumar-is-my-idol-amitabh-bachchan-3040.html
10. http://timesofindia.indiatimes.com/entertainment/hindi/bollywood/news/Amitabh-Bachchan-remembers-Hrishikesh-Mukherjee-as-a-genius/articleshow/44002853.cms

11. http://indiatoday.intoday.in/story/a-tribute-by-amitabh-bachchan/1/292940.html
12. http://srbachchan.tumblr.com/post/25143256739
13. http://www.rediff.com/movies/report/big-b-suffers-from-hernia-to-undergo-surgery/20100504.htm
14. https://www.elitecolumn.com/amitabh-bachchan-injury-conquered/amitabh-bachchan-l4-5-damage/
15. http://movies.ndtv.com/bollywood/amitabh-bachchan-after-deewar-my-mother-wept-like-a-child-646409
16. http://www.rediff.com/movies/2003/oct/11ab.htm
17. www.rediff.com/movies/1999/may/12ab.htm
18. http://indianexpress.com/article/entertainment/bollywood/amitabh-bachchan-opens-memorial-trust-in-fathers-name/
19. http://timesofindia.indiatimes.com/entertainment/hindi/bollywood/news/Amitabh-Bachchan-I-suffered-from-TB-in-2000/articleshow/45598810.cms
20. https://www.linkedin.com/pulse/3-things-i-learnt-from-amitabh-bachchan-harjeet-khanduja
21. http://www.mid-day.com/articles/big-b-nostalgia-trip/83031
22. https://www.filmcomment.com/article/the-rise-and-fall-and-rebirth-of-bollywood-superstar-amitabh-bachchan/
23. http://www.hindustantimes.com/brunch/amitabh-bachchan-has-stood-the-test-of-time-karan-johar/story-KeohOQXVDJsRdiPyo6NfiK.html
24. https://en.wikiquote.org/wiki/Amitabh_Bachchan
25. http://blogs.siliconindia.com/Amitabhbachchan/DAY_741_Amitabh_Bachchan_Blog-bid-4w7V8hDF73992521.html//education/

Manufactured by Amazon.ca
Bolton, ON

36809611R00074